All Around Us:

Poems from the Valley

All Around Us:

Poems from the Valley

Linda Parsons and Candance W. Reaves, Editors

A Poetry Anthology from the Knoxville Writers' Guild

Blue Ridge Publishing
Emerald House Group, Inc.
Greenville, South Carolina

1996

ISBN: 1-889893-00-5
Copyright © 1996 by Blue Ridge Publishing
All Around Us: Poems from the Valley

Printed in USA

Published by
Blue Ridge Publishing
Emerald House Group, Inc.
1 Chick Springs Road, Suite 206
Greenville, SC 29609

******

Knoxville Writers' Guild
P.O. Box 10326
Knoxville, TN 37939

Cover:
Cold Mountain © 1979 Barry Spann
Graphite on Paper, 5" x 7 3/4"
Private Collection

Design/Desktop Publishing: Mark Perryman
Printing: EBSCO Media/Debbie Patton Hollenbeck

In memory of Libba Moore Gray,
whose heart dances in beauty
all around us.

March 3, 1937–June 3, 1995

May it be beautiful before me.
May it be beautiful behind me.
May it be beautiful below me.
May it be beautiful above me.
May it be beautiful all around me.
In beauty it is finished.

—from the Navajo Night Chant

ACKNOWLEDGMENTS

In a community of emerging writers' groups and their inevitable desire to publish collected works, we gratefully acknowledge the board of the Knoxville Writers' Guild for supporting the development of this anthology. By allowing the poets of this region—the widely published and the unsung—their particular place on the page and the bookshelf, the Guild performs an invaluable service to the writing community. We are grateful to Robert Gray for lending us Libba's name and a selection of poems so that her presence can enrich this book and regional talent can be recognized with the annual Libba Moore Gray Poetry Prize. The Department of English at the University of Tennessee, Knoxville, in particular Dr. Allen Carroll, was generous in supporting both the anthology and contributing the Young Writer's Prize, the winners of which are published in this volume. We thank Dr. Marilyn Kallet for giving us our wonderful title, her support of this project, and her continuing leadership as gentle caryatid of the arts locally, statewide, and beyond. Our thanks go to *The Knoxville News-Sentinel*, especially Diana Morgan and Fred Brown, who were enormously helpful in publicity and encouragement as we organized the poetry competitions and developed the anthology. Barry Spann is proud to see his work grace this gathering of East Tennessee poets, and we're delighted with his generosity and our beautiful cover. Emily Anderson and Kathy Hall also were invaluable in our search for the right cover. We greatly appreciate Jeff Daniel Marion and John Reaves for their patience, love, wise counsel, and unbeatable proofreading skills. For pitching in near the end, we are grateful to Marcia Lawson, who created an electronic version of the manuscript for the publisher. Finally, more than we can say, we applaud the poets who submitted work for consideration and the voices gracing the collection—they have led us into necessary darkness, they have affirmed our place in the light, they have sung us lullabies, they have jarred us awake. They have set us on the ground we walk toward home, where the waiting world shimmers all around us. Thank you one and all.

PREFACE

We met on a spring morning in 1993, Libba Moore Gray and I. She served tea and we talked across a small bouquet of primroses, hyacinths, and periwinkles that decorated a cozy wooden booth in her Knoxville home. There, she told me about her life, her writing...her battles with cancer. It was a meeting both exhilarating and difficult. Exhilarating because I knew I was in the presence of an energetic, attractive woman who would make "great copy" for the newspaper story I was writing about her first book. Difficult because there was *so much story* there, and much of it was alarming. How to portray Libba in print was a question much on my mind, for to spend an hour with this singular woman was to become acquainted with a whole host of Libbas. In the end, I was reduced to cataloging this woman who had been so many women...*wife, mother, grandmother, actress, teacher, dancer, children's author, cancer-fighter, poet...*

Above all, perhaps, she was a poet.

She was more well known as actress, dancer, and teacher—roles that drew upon her magnetic personality and ability as a performer. Still, a poetic sensibility fed everything she did, whether telling jokes and stories to her four children, starring in plays such as *The Taming of the Shrew* and *The Glass Menagerie* or serving as a symbol of hope for cancer survivors.

Libba could lift the spirits of an audience of hundreds—or an audience of one—even when her body and soul needed lifting. I've seen her enter an auditorium on crutches in order to give a speech, following hours of grueling medical procedures. Yet when the lights came on at the podium, it was her smile, her voice, her generous words that illuminated the room, drawing all eyes to hers. She basked in such attention.

Libba always loved an encore, and in her scary and glorious and existential autumn she had lots of them, especially as a writer of children's books. Her ongoing dance with death renewed her commitment to write. I've watched her at work.

She takes her next breath, she writes down some words.

Inhale. Exhale. A brief choreography of fingers.

Libba Moore Gray was grateful for such transactions.

"I wanted to leave something for my students and grandchildren to remember me by," she said that first day. It had taken a while for the rest of the world to catch on. She sent several stories to publishers of children's books without a sale, she said. Then one day her sister, Suzanne, reminded her of the stories Libba used to tell her babies many years ago about a woman named *Miss Tizzy*. Libba committed the story to paper, little knowing it would become her first book. Between her diagnosis of breast cancer in 1989 and her death on June 3, 1995, she saw five books published and acclaimed. More have been published since.

To turn the pages of those books is to hear a jingle and a jangle of musical rhythm and wordplay. But then, her poetic sensibility showed up everywhere and sometimes more somberly. Take this entry from her personal journal:

Nov. 27, 1989: I walked through piles of colored leaves. Strands of my hair went sailing on the wind…Maybe the birds use hair in their nests…

Libba was forever pointing out the mystery and poetry inherent in the world. How a cardinal she had seen perched atop a building found its way, mysteriously, into an illustration for *Miss Tizzy*. How her children's stories foreshadowed and illuminated her own battles with cancer. How her journey through physical disintegration paralleled the travels and travails of a certain *Little Black Truck*. How she drew meaning from injustices against *Dear Willie Rudd,* the black housekeeper who tended her as a child.

Some of her poetic gifts doubtlessly came from Willie Rudd.

"I remember mostly her strength and the spirituals she used to sing to me," Libba told me. "She was this beautiful, ebony black."

Some of the rhythms and imagery in her writings were gifts from a far-flung family of storytellers and other characters from her childhood in Virginia. Libba left behind fragments of a novel about those people.

Wherever it came from, Libba's poetic voice made itself manifest early on. When she was twelve she entered a contest on the radio. The prize was a doll popular in the 1950s named "Sparkle Plenty." The girl who submitted the best letter telling why she deserved to own the doll would win one.

"I wrote this letter that was so pitiful that I won," Libba said. "That's when I learned the power of words. I should have known then that I was a writer, but I chose theater." She studied ballet and modern dance as a child, then majored in English and drama at Emory & Henry and later Carson-Newman College, where she completed her formal education.

She taught school from the early 1970s, mostly at Heritage High in Blount County. But more than her teaching, more than her dancing and acting and formal poetry, her children's books, in those last years, provided purpose.

"These books are my 'Gift of the Magi,' " she said, referring to a classic Christmas story by O. Henry. But another O. Henry story comes to mind, and reference to it made its way into my first newspaper article about Libba. The story is "The Last Leaf." It concerns a deathly ill woman who watches leaves fall, one by one, from a tree outside her window. When the last leaf falls, she fears, she too will die. But one leaf hangs on, day after day.

Like that leaf, Libba's writing persevered in the face of illness, although in the end neither medical science nor perseverance as a writer could keep Libba living. But all who knew her, and who take solace in her poetry, are grateful for the courage and the will to write which fed each other in those final years.

It is gratifying to write the preface for a book that enshrines the memory of this woman beloved by so many. A book which brings together a substantial sampling of her pure poetry, which you may judge or enjoy as you wish. Someday her collected poems will be published. In the meantime, try these. Also included here is verse by winners of the first annual Libba Moore Gray Poetry Prize, bestowed by the Knoxville Writers' Guild. She would be pleased, I think.

As I say, Libba always loved an encore.

—Don Williams
June 30, 1996

When many people think of poetry, they remember a day in the fourth grade where they stood in front of the class, nervous and ramrod straight, for their recitation of Longfellow. And perhaps in college, poetry was little more than romantic yearnings from the English countryside which, seemingly, had no relation to their daily lives. With this anthology, we want to bring poetry back into your reach, your thinking, your lives. We want to make poetry as accessible and necessary to you as music or fine food.

It's a truism that we overlook what's right under our noses. In fact, we often discount the beauty of our personal landscape and place more value on the distant and exotic. A handful of gravel from your own driveway tumbled and polished by a jeweler would be unrecognizable as something so ordinary. The same is true for the poems in this volume. They're gathered from the driveways we pass every day, the ordinary houses and rooms and yards that lie all around us waiting to be noticed and held to the light.

In the search to fill these pages and to honor regional poets, the Knoxville Writers' Guild created two annual contests—the Libba Moore Gray Poetry Prize and the Young Writer's Prize, chosen from area high school juniors and seniors. We proudly feature the winners of both. And we just as proudly dedicate the book to the memory of Libba Moore Gray, whose spirit infuses every line. Also included is work solicited from well-loved and respected writers such as Marilyn Kallet, George Scarbrough, Jeff Daniel Marion, Arthur Smith, and Connie Jordan Green. Equally rewarding to us were the surprises that arrived in the mail from poets who have labored alone in their private journey, but whose voices beat with a force no longer unheard. These poets, great and small, bring you the earnest heat of their skill and sing you the work of the living, open-throated and full.

The anthology begins with summer and the power of memory, where fireflies spark all that's beautiful and difficult from our childhoods, where cicadas become petaled wings that carry us into what we must bear as adults. The seasons of all our days follow: the poets see love come and go from their lives, discuss pumpkins and red leaves and the secrets of seeds, spin their fables like shawls over the graying of winter as well as their hair, wish for home of heart and hills, tear down fences that divide—piece by peace, mourn those who taught us to live well and not go gentle into that good night, witness the greening of hope and spring, and dream their dreams already in the future. Above all, they dance through language, fresh and strong at every turn, shouting down the dark, seeing what is bitter and sweet all around us, and letting us taste of their tree of life.

We hope you'll love and admire these poems as much as we do and that you'll seek out more poetry after reading this book. You may see rocks in your driveway differently now. You may even hear the rooms in your house speaking to you, urging you to remember people and places long forgotten. Stop and listen to them; carry a stone for luck in your pocket. Hear and see the poetry in your morning cup of coffee and in the changing light of evening. It's a world as close as your own backyard.

—*Linda Parsons*
Candance W. Reaves

CONTENTS

xx

IV. The Work of the Living

I

Their Presence So Light

MARILYN KALLET

Fireflies

In the dry summer field at nightfall,
fireflies rise like sparks.
Imagine the presence of ghosts
flickering, the ghosts of young friends,
your father nearest in the distance.
This time they carry no sorrow,
no remorse, their presence is so light.
Childhood comes to you,
memories of your street in lamplight,
holding those last moments before bed,
capturing lightning bugs,
with a blossom of the hand
letting them go. Lightness returns,
an airy motion over the ground
you remember from *ring-around-the-rosie.*
If you stay, the fireflies become fireflies
again, not part of your stories,
as unaware of you as sleep, being
beautiful and quiet all around you.

LISA COFFMAN

The Cicadas

Of constant things, they are most constant,
inciting memory, never the thing remembered
but the attendant, bordering the way into memory,
girls strewing petals the day of the wedding

within veils of wings. Hear the pattern to the confusion:
something fumbled for, and dropped, and fumbled for,
the right bead slipped on a string. A thread apparent,
a limb. The summer night is always dimmed

by the woman in her slip at the window,
car headlights on the dark stain of the river
extinguished, and other light scattered on the river
the way memory obstructs a certain dark—

The ring of children has scattered. They hide
and glitter, small lungs spreading, folding.
Already the first call back *safe! home!*
Now you can bear to remember what you

could bear to do, once, carried by breathing
so like this music, in which what you lose, recurs.
The scale of the night slowly fills with petals,
leaves edged in weak light, the laboring wings.

4

DANIEL ROOP

The Next

    for Katherine

Galway for a boy, *Xan* for a girl—it began with names,
rising in our personal mythology like sun-warmth across
a galaxy to mean *love* and *god.* Our children, years away
from conception, blazed into existence over a phone line
the first time we talked, took up permanent residence
in my mind, pushed out dust words, promised new ones
as musical as sweat on our backs that will create their perfect bodies.
Old life is no longer enough as I look to the next,
to our first act of creation and worship, this new language in seed
we will half-teach them, they will be half-born with,
a vocabulary past sleep and death. I don't yet have the breath
for it, dream of the day you will take me by my wrist, pulses joining
as you lead me to our children's room, like the promise of you
drawing me from the womb years ago, whisper as you
open their door, *Here, let me show you.*

Second Place
Libba Moore Gray Poetry Prize

5

LINDA PARSONS

My Daughter's Feet

Years ago, before you stood alone,
you melted like mints in my mouth.
Were you ever that new, before hopscotch,
before *fudge, fudge, tell the judge?*
Were you ever that easy to catch?
Pink and smooth-heeled, you were
pebbles sipping moonlight. You were
Gretel's crumbs, and Gretel, racing
wood and hawk and changeling night.

ACEY NEEL

My Mother, the Bees (and Me)

My mother, young and blond and beautiful,
Stretched high off the ground to catch a quick glimpse
Of honey bees: plump, fat and yellow while
They feasted on the sweet, sticky delight.
Protected by a thick, white layer of
Heavy cotton overalls, gloves and mask,
My mother reached carefully in the tree,
Grasping for their stingers, felt the kick of
A child, developing fingers and toes
To the rhythm of a thousand buzzes.

Honorable Mention
Young Writer's Prize

EDWARD FRANCISCO

Winter Vision

From his window view
my son seizes
a ribbon of morning light
that gives him
excuse to pause, take
measure of the ochre mist
shrouding the still-dark presences
of trees.

He's riddled in his chest
by the sight of rocks
splitting the sun's head, now
a wobble on the mountain's
trembling shoulders.

Snow dies in gasps around us.

We listen for the whistle of doves' wings.

Within that liquid trail
of light are country dwellers.
And what is left of morning
is the snarl of wood smoke
curling from a neighbor's
chimney—rock upon rock—laid
with a Neanderthal's precision.

No fire could ever destroy
what those hands have stacked.

Still tasting the trailing nectar
of light, my son touches
the window lace of frost
and asks, "What is a poem?"
A duck bobs its drenched feathers
on a startled pond.

"A poem's the face you
make when no one's looking."

We smile with smiles
yellow as old photographs.

At ten, he confesses to a heart
that is comic and sly.

To both our liking is a dream
of solid ground and the frenzied
thawing of possibilities unearthed
by accident.

Now gutters tick
like a metronome.

Even fog can't conceal
the spot where a crow
flies its crooked smile.

FLORENCE McNABB

A Pause

Driving home from work on the last
day of November I'm wishing for thirty-
one and repeat the old rhyme
once again. OK, I relent at last,
as I'm sucked into a yellow wake
of leaves from the car ahead, lighting
up the six o'clock dark.
I search for leaves still on trees
along the road. Pin oaks sometimes
keep their leaves until May,
when the new growth just pushes
them off. It's only a number, thirty,
a way to mark time. But,
the last! We check each month like milk
on a shopping list. Well, we can't
mark the day we'll die, and that day
exists! Every year it comes
and goes unrecognized. I've
had forty-four deathdays.
If I knew mine I would celebrate
with cake and blow the candles on
instead of out. Seems like
we do it backwards. Anyway,
Mr. Newton will be eighty-nine
tomorrow, the first day
of December and so many more to come,
days that don't need counting. So I'll let
go of November, a notch in time's
passing, and forge on, like my car
up the driveway now, where the headlights
shine briefly on a tree in the woods,
a pin oak maybe, its full body
of leaves glistening in the night.

CANDANCE W. REAVES

One by One

Like Scheherazade
he tells his stories one by one,
of wonders like wildflowers
and waterfalls in distant gorges,
gemlike trout in deep blue pools
appearing like djinn
and gone in a whisper,
of copper beeches and silverbells,
revealing them slowly
as if he dares not reach
the climax
for fear I'll disappear
by morning.

Like Othello
he weaves the round unvarnished tale
of close escapes
and scrapes and bruises,
broken spirits
and forgiveness—
but only bits so not to frighten or appall
or fall from grace
or see my face show
pity, no.

Like himself
he tells the tales so well
that no one,
not one,
could tell them in his place.

That Girl

for Libba, who would have loved her

How could one have told her
We make too much of unkind inlaws
And doting hags too daft for anything
But taking sides?

How have explained to her
She needed no extra help,
No intramural intervention?
That renownless work belies

Great expectations?
That time and circumstance
Do not contend against us?
And all those other small-time

Profundities we sometimes
Win our way with?
Words would have failed,
She was so sunken

In her own self-pity
And the believed fastness
Of a fixed overlordship.
The morning the Prince came,

Her hair strung, and her nails,
Both hand and foot, were dirty.
Moreover, buttons were missing
And her slip showed.

No wonder, losing his footing
On the puddled floor,
He wrinkled his nose in disdain.
The swollen mess of sour milk

Drawing flies on the windowsill
Did not help matters. The Prince
Waved them away. "Better,"
He remarked, "to dismiss the girl

Than suffer this."
"One has one's responsibility,"
The Stepmother whined,
"Especially to family. Blood

Is thicker than soup, you know."
"Surely thicker than her soup,"
A willing sister chimed in.
The clock on the mantel chimed.

It was eleven o'clock exactly.
The girl was consuming her sixth
Slice of souse by that time,
And her hands were greasy.

Dipping them into the sudsy pail
Beside her, she saw them come away
Dripping with bits of rainbow.
Charmed, she thought of the palace

Jewels and lifted gobs of foam
To her young breasts,
Dabbed them at her earlobes,
Strung them in a radiant arc

Of bubbles across her frowzy hair.
In a scrap of dropped mirror
She got one galvanized look
Before a playful doorway wind

Blew all away.
But transformation had occurred.
Not because she had it coming or
That in any way it was inevitable,

But because she was lucky:
Right time, right scenario.
She became a born-again woman.
The rest was easy.

ART STEWART

In Their Time

As a young child, He resurrected birds from the dead.
They shook themselves alive and sprang into the air
frightened but glad to live again.

　　　Somewhere, I once read
that less than two nanoseconds after the Big Bang
all physical laws of the universe had already
leaped out of the incredible

spark of nothing to hold
center stage full-blown: the jester's
two-toned hat had bells, the bull's
big balls hung to his hairy knees.

But uncertainty crept in. Pan
began looking for his lost pipes while Pandora
began writing and rewriting the script for patience.
Athena worked in her kitchen baking bread;

she was kneading and kneading the dough to learn Zen
when suddenly she came to an ecstatic state of
enlightenment and everything began running
backwards, spilling time into the aisles,

making hills, then mountains, of chaos.
In dreamland I recreate the universe:
I begin putting things gently into their places
one by one a long night I tell myself

all things will come in their time.

CONNIE JORDAN GREEN

Cinderella Reflects

It is years since I have been there—
the house like a box,
sharp corners capturing dirt,
windows like eyes
where I polished away all flaws.
And the fireplace—
ash-tipped poker
heavy as oak logs,
handle I kept bright as the windows,
hearth clean as purity.

Years since I've seen the family—
sister who reviled me,
mother who saw only
my back, my arms, muscles
meant to ease her days.

The dance freed me—
gown of tulle and taffeta
fashioned from wish and desire,
delicate shoes
fitted to feet
hobbled by years of custom,
freedom stolen in childhood.

The house, the family—
they are still there
but I go only in memory,
the pall that covers me
when night comes—
midnight my distant dream.

JENNY NASH

The Virgin Queen

The pure and empty vessel, haunting to
be filled. I am Elizabeth, the first
daughter of the bastard church, taunting you
and kings with my virginity, but cursed
with lessons of love learned early at my
headless mother's knee. Lessons imbedded
deeper in my child's soul by Katherine's cry
at the block. This vessel, needing dreaded
love poured like a balm over raw edges,
teases and flirts closer to the abyss,
peering into the soft blackness, then hedges
all bets with gold—not flesh but my kiss.
I am Elizabeth, never to bed
any man, knowing the price is my head.

STACY SMITH

Flowers Not for Touching

Long-spined trunks of men
rise around me,
their backs pushing up toward true light
like eager, open sunflowers,
seeds ripe and arousing flight.
I press my cheek
against beds of seed,
petals throw yellow light upon sunlight
on my waiting face.

Nodding stalk spines
affirm, affirm,
I am woman.
Yes-rocking heads rocking *yes* stir the chains—
Circles and circles,
link after thumb-wide link
to children,
the wife in a life of ties
already made, sweet,
precious as roots
claiming them away—

JOHN IRVIN

The First Mother

Before the suppressing rays of day
lay down on darkness of nature,
a black crossed the woodland path.
A black what?
A black woman.
Keen in sense and wild like the berries
growing under her feet
may be why she tasted so exotic.
But the beasts never questioned the taste.
They just licked and loved and
made music in the night.
No sight, only the rustling sound
of the trees swaying and banging
and becoming one within themselves.
But when the light peeked
over the mountaintop
all of the creatures were gone.
All except the black.
The black what?
The black woman.
Covered in her red blood
and green leaves that lived
and bananas which
had fallen from above.
Yellow so bright
heaven was speaking to her.
God spoke, "You are my sister,
my daughter, the holy ghost.
I show you the seed from the
most savage forest so you
may tame the pain by showing love.
I share with you the knowledge:
hate dies after death but
love lives forever."
Hearing, feeling, and living
this experience

the first mother smeared her blood
across her body and tied
the bananas around her neck
along with the green leaves
around her hips.
On her voyage the four colors
would represent her:
red, yellow, green, and the black.
The black what?
The black woman

First Place
Young Writer's Prize

LIBBA MOORE GRAY

August

In August the earth is selfish
shimmers   bakes brown   hardens
like a veined woman stretched flat in the sun...
she shifts...groans
calls to the priests for sacrifice...
the women dance the rain dance
naked   steaming with sweat
their hair streaming down   sticking to their breasts
and still they dance and relief does not come...
their bodies beat
beating a rhythm as old as the sun bearing down on them
and the earth gives and moves and cracks beneath their feet
and the jeweled fingers of the crepe myrtle tremble
from the feet beating on the earthdrum...
and the dance goes on and on
until the orchard floors are covered with the fallen fruit
shaken loose by the dance...
skin of peach split wide open draining sweetness
into a ground always thirsting for more
and the dancers move and turn and throb to the beat
until the bleeding feet   stop
and the dancers fall exhausted among the bruised fruit...
their breathing slows   soon stops...
the holy stillness broken only by the liquid crying
of a raincrow lamenting the fallen dancers
the sky darkens   grows black
in the fermenting fruit the wild jackals stop
read the dark canopy of clouds
sniff the dampness in the air
while in the distance the faint sound of thunder rides the wind.

BRIAN GRIFFIN

His Last Tales

Perhaps the tales were fiction, as though
at death our lives give way to fable:

    Of how the bees in spring
    would gather in clover
    beside the springhouse of a farm
    of selfish people, well enough off.
    And how the boys, sneaking there
    to steal a hoop of cheese
    or shank of beef, might press
    their bare and calloused feet
    onto a laden bee or two,
    gorging on a white and hidden blossom.
    Such pain, he said, was
    something one must bear.

    Or of the time when,
    taken with worn tales
    of love and riches,
    he introduced a vagabond
    as Cousin Alf from Milledgeville,
    and gained him supper and a bed,
    for neither Mom nor Dad
    (too busy to confer)
    would dare to question
    one another's kin.
    And how in deep blue moonlight,
    the drifter smoked a pipe
    outside the barn
    and paid the boy with lies
    about life's wonders,
    and gave him his first shot
    of hobo whiskey.
    Then, under the spell
    of stories and stars,
    the boy rose up, just high enough

above that bitter earth,
to see what lay beyond
the Georgia fields:
the way big cities reeled in
miles of promise; the way
true love might wait beside
the ocean, for a while.
The morning brought
a pilfered drawer of silver,
the drifter's straw bed bare
and cleared of hope.

Were such tales his way to stake a claim
to a world that would not share an acre?

No matter—for he was interrupted by the nurses
who brought their arm cuffs, vials and silver needles,
as though the need that plagued him for so long
could be beaten back by science, even now.
He stared away; they nudged him back;
his days passed into nothing,
until at last his mind denied it all
and claimed its space in spite of all like me:

That's when he picked the fruit
that called to him, oranges so plentiful
they nudged the very grass that graced his bed,
and grapes as large as life could ever be.
He raised his twig-bent arms into the air,
vacant to all time-bound eyes like mine,
and in his yellowed eyes, even in their age,
I saw a child who could not bear the loss,
nor stand at last the pain of tiny stings—
who ran, as all would do in such a state,
to find some loving arms to pull him in.

CAROLINE NORRIS

Tulip Greeting

We buried my mother-in-law on a mild
May morning. I heard insects sing and voices murmur,
felt the sun. Felt nothing. Along the path
beside the drive, red tulips bowed and curtseyed.
Nodding politely to the dead, I thought.
We stood straight, the boys and I, caught
in stiff appropriate poses, while hurt, need,
anger were buried in the sludge and aftermath
of death. No way now to confirm her
hatred; no way for charges to be filed

or accusations made. The time for hearts to bleed
was over. "A woman of integrity,"
someone intoned—of rigidity, one might say,
of dull perfections—biscuits puffed higher
than mine, a son too smart for me—"She gave
her life to others, faced illness with brave
calm"—wonder if souls face fire
from angels itching to reward them one bright day
for little snidenesses? If there's celebrity
status for people who take lifetimes to concede?

Huge cloud as convoluted as the brain of God
sailed high, cutting the slant of sun
on turned soil. A small hand slipped into mine.
Perhaps she's laughing at me still.
I can't know; will not knowing
drive me crazy? Is this woman going
to haunt me? For an instant I felt ill
then sensed the sun emerge and shine
and realized she will not. I've finally won.
I heard the lovely sound of falling sod.

And yet…is death some sort of haven for the dead,
some hiding place too secret, too exquisite
for mortals? She'll eye me while I'm making jam

with that slight lip curl, not quite criticism
not open at all, not really a sneer,
yet speaking volumes in language just as clear
as ordinary words. Tongue ready with some witticism
to deprecate. Well, Mama, here I am,
ready at last. "Mother, will Gramma come to visit
us?"

I looked down fondly. "No," I said.

ART STEWART

First-Up Man

It was Grandad who taught me to be a
first-up man in love with water. The rattle of early
wood and stove would wake me each time, a
flood of little noises. At first

I would try to snuggle deeper into bed while he
pulled on his boots, put on his jacket and took
down his gooseneck shovel, all
business. Hard stars held the dark

sky as cold as a desert. When he walked
he was almost as lean as his shovel. Sometimes he would
stop, tilt his head to the left, look down at his
rough hands and quote clean lines

I thought then from Frost: "I never saw so much swift water
run cloudless, the stream of everything that runs away.
Blood, though, is harder to dam back than water,
and carries the code one must obey."

When I stepped out into the first
dark morning with him to practice the art of water,
the sky in the east was a thin
sliver of orange.

He slipped the heavy boards into the head-box and
pounded them into place to force the water up.
Eighty acre-feet would come, steadied by his eye:
like a god he stood

guiding the water down a hundred
long rows of cotton. Within each row, the bed
plants stood perfect, a black line in a silver stream.
"The blood of the earth is water," he said.

For a moment only
we stood wet together on bank side
listening just to the gurgle of water, the sun
creeping up over the dark mountains.

Third Place
Libba Moore Gray Poetry Prize

CANDANCE W. REAVES

Grandmother

A scarred brown photo says she rode sidesaddle
and wore split leather skirts.
My mother hardly remembers the angel
my grandfather so adored.
Uncle John never knew her.
He sang her deathsong from the womb.

Her heart was fragile
and the doctor miles away
when the boy she had longed for
slid into the light
and she to the night
where there are no mornings.
The strength of his living could not hold her.
She left him howling and blinking
while two sisters waited stiffly on the sofa
for some word.

JOAN SHROYER-KENO

Knowing

Crickets, feather pillow,
old soft sheets against my cheek.
My mother, does she sleep
or turn and bend fourteen
hours on the night shift?
My grandmother curled
on her side, snoring. My great
grandmother flat on her
back. Stomach rising, falling.
Like her mother and her mother
before her: rising, blooming,
enduring, falling back to earth.
I see them in their fields, kitchens,
factories. Under their moon-white
sheets darned and bleached
their eyes in darkness, blinking.
Each seeing the lives their mothers
longed for, but never had.

SANDRA CANNON

The Storyteller

My grandmother has a storeroom full of stories.
Some sad.
Some long.
Some about family.
Most about herself.
She tells her stories
and asks us to believe in truths & tall tales,
to understand Jim Crow, 40 acres & a mule,
reconstruction, emancipation.
She asks us to believe
as she spins her tales from golden threads of folklore.
She sews communal quilts, you know.
Patterned wedding rings, figure eights, and such.
Tales about walking five miles to school
one way
passing the white folks' school on the way
down lanes & up hills & over purple-flowered valleys
to the one-room schoolhouse
where she matriculated for 8 straight years
graduating at the top of her class
of 6.
Straightway
she smiles
remembering her mother & father &
blackberry pie &
penny this & nickel that &
clotheslines & washboards &
church socials & river baptisms &
whippings meted out to sassy children who had a
mind of their own.
A mind of her own
is what my grandmother had...
now the old timers' disease has clouded
a memory once keen
once sharp
once upon a grand time
when my grandmother was my storyteller.

WILLIAM H. P. NEVILS

A Summer Reflection

The days are long, soft and deep.
We carve the hours to make of what we wish.
We seek cooling waters and teas,
ices of raspberry, lemon and lime.
We speak slowly to brown white men and women
in bonnets and hats of straw,
as if, unto us only, was the gift of time.

We eat outside.
The breeze has lain upon the lawn.
Watermelons are heavy and ripe.
We linger, like the strollers
on a *Sunday Afternoon on the Island of Grand Jatte*
by Georges Pierre Seurat.
The jarflies chatter in shady groves
on the edge of the sun.
"The 'periodic cicada'!" we say,
laughing at what we know.

Birdsong rings, somnolent in the heat,
red birds over the open calm to
sleeping doves in their sequestered willow bower.
Grandmothers and great-great uncles and aunts
tell us how wonderful we are—
a love, familiar, as flowered and faded cotton.
Andrew is "pretty as a peach."
The girls are "like a picture."
New friendships seem old,
old ones, are still forever.

Late warm suppers welcome us
in a cool kitchen.
Outside, fireflies from the boxwoods rising
heft the twilight with softer light
and skim the treetops.

Our imaginations quicken and soar
with these fragile joys,
for only there will they ever be
precisely the same again,
or perhaps,
in summers yet unbegotten
or other distant eyes
who have not yet seen to see.

MELISSA THOMPSON

The Visitor

Wind chimes dangle above the open porch
where the lawn is dust over dry blades.
A woman's laundry dries alone
spreading across sky.
One towel.
One pillowcase.

In the morning, the sink begins with
a teacup—small coffee ring
in its base.
Things are new here.
There is a chance of visitors
or the one for
whom the pillowcase
flaps on the line.

At noon
she almost hears the neighbor children
playing a mile away.
The empty can rattles over gravel when kicked,
they chant *Tag*
You're it.
By evening something inside begins to dim.
She will light a candle by
the open window.
He may see it down the road.

Waiting is drinking the last of the lemonade
when you are still thirsty.
Water cannot satisfy after that.
The sink is empty now and
by midnight her eyes will close.
The body will say it is time for sleep.
The heart will say,
Wait, wait.

STACY SMITH

Dreaming My Daughter

for Michael: who is like God

She is born,
my daughter without a name.
Before her birth
I dreamed her living,
an elf in the back of my mind
playing with blocks, tumbling in the grass.

Now she lives,
she is my constant companion.
I carry her to the ski lodge
every day, trying each time
to bundle her warmly enough,
her hands and legs and arms increasing in size exponentially.

She feeds me,
this tiny woman,
her blond curls springing forth with power.
I hold her all day and notice
to the others at the lodge
we've become a unit.
They watch this mother,
shoulders turned in on her infant daughter,
this knowing, this loving every second,
this person who has overcome me, made me an "us" once again.

Earlier today I saw her walk,
bending and stretching
against the too-small creeper that fit her
just this morning,
her head full to bursting from
the knit cap I topped her with.

This afternoon I carried her
along the cement walkway by the river,

all the merchants
looking at her with longing,
wanting her to be their next poster child
for playground equipment or office machines.

This evening she grew to four
and began talking to me in adult language.
Courtney! Courtney! I called, laughing.
Is that my name? she asked me.
I stood dumb before the sudden words of my child.
I told her I've called her
Alicia and Courtney,
both gray in my mind, neither seeming to name her.
I look to this standing child of four
and begin to form apologies
for going so long
without giving her a name.
Before I can speak
she says she was a boy before she was born,
playing outside with boys and blocks.
Her friends' names were Alex
(great protector) and Drew (trustworthy).
And my name was Michael. I like that name.

JEFF CALLAHAN

Ten

Tedium of long drives at night when you're ten
and there's nothing to look at and nothing to do
and a heaping dose of nothing on the radio.

Beyond the lighted dash the land is still and flat
as a smashed plate of food, only the treeline blurring past
the windows and the hard glare of oncoming traffic.

You ask your father what it's like to be dead.
He counsels you to think of it as a change and not
an end, a kind of new beginning, but you're ten

so you're skeptical, and now it's raining and the air
smells horribly like sulphur as you cross a rusty bridge
high above some ruined river caught like

a wounded animal in the distant lights of Port Arthur.
You look at your mother and sister asleep in the back.
Is *that* what it's like to be dead? You don't think so.

You imagine your own funeral and the look
on your parents' faces as they file past your coffin,
your mother's face composed in the Greek mask

of tragedy you saw once at school, until your father
ruffles your hair with his hand and you want to say,
Stop, goddammit, I'm dead, but you're ten so you don't.

What you offer instead is silence and a big fat smirk,
which is about all you're good for when you're ten
and you're bored and you're stuck in a car in east Texas.

FLORENCE McNABB

Grazing Their Wings

For weeks pigeons thatched my grandmother's roof,
        blanketed the ground beneath the kiosk-
shaped birdfeeder on stilts, just beyond the flagstone patio.
    Back then, my description might have been:
Hundreds of gross, fat birds lurked on Grandmother's roof,

            waiting to swoop down and pluck out her eyes when
    she filled the feeder. Twenty years from *lurked* and *pluck* to *thatched*
            and *blanketed,* from Hitchcockian suspense and gore to
the polished and unexciting. A green horse finally broken, my sister
    might insert here, unasked, unwelcome.

Will you drive me to the liquor store? Yes, Grandmother, aware
        that the best way to get an explanation was by not
asking for one. *I want the strongest liquor you sell,* she announced
        to the clerks who stared as an eighty-five-year-old
and an underage drove away with a quart of Pure Grain, a million proof.

32

        She poured the alcohol into a Pyrex lasagna pan filled
with Pepperidge Farm breadcrumbs, and we watched them soak
        the liquor up. To my silence she said, *When the pigeons*
eat the bread they'll get drunk and won't be able to fly, then I can just
        pick them up and place them nicely in the garbage.

Besides pigeons the fumes kept all creatures away—from the bread,
        the feeder, the roof, the yard—for a week until the alcohol
evaporated. The titmice were the first to return, one or two daily,
        then the regulars, purple finches, grosbeaks, chickadees,
and the pigeons, their ranks now reinforced, doubled in number.

    Next, chicken wire six feet high around the entire area.
The feeder became an Alcatraz for pigeons breaking in, breaking out.
        The ball-peen hammer for banging on the sliding glass
door lost its fright power. Then, the request for my BB gun. *Sure,*
Grandmother! thinking, *she'd never cock it.* Still,

every pigeon and his brother, she would say, was in her yard. One day
        standing at her front door I heard—*thfit thfit thfit.* I let
myself in and saw her at the patio door re-cocking the gun, its nose

waving wildly in the air, her lips pursed in their perpetual
whistle. She was under five feet tall standing there in high heels dyed

   royal blue to match the flecks of blue in her linen suit, her blue
satin blouse with its floppy bow at the neck, a blue velvet hat on her head
   semi-circled with a band of feathers, the mottled colors
of an obscure bird, maybe a harlequin pigeon, like the ones that stood out
   in the blue-green flock, the *gross ones,* I might have said then.

I'm just grazing their wings, she said to my surprised face, *to stun them a bit.*
   At the time I humored that little lady who actually believed she had
hit the wings of birds with a gun she could barely lift. Thinking then,
   grandmother, old, eccentric. Now thinking, *vital, exciting,*
Hitchcock's distant cousin. A green horse unbreakable, my sister
   might say here, a more than welcome insertion.

Honorable Mention
Libba Moore Gray Poetry Prize

EDWARD FRANCISCO

On Being Photographed in Middle Age

By no means now the boy in the striped shirt
I was at ten—he
hangs on the upstairs wall, object
of passing curiosity but more of derision
by this laughing house of children
who wonder why he never smiles.
I don't tell them he had no reason

or that he'd probably just been beaten
by a tense mother never agreeing
with the way he tucked his shirt in
(worse than an orphan, she said)
or combed his hair back off his head.
Same boy tried for years to locate just
the right crease in his clothes, the right
style to satisfy the unsatisfiable requirements
of one not pictured.

Not even the slender likeness taken
in college where he dressed the part
of a protester without a protest, without
a word of his own, could conceal
the borrowed texts under his arm
enabling him to quote someone else's
pain by proxy, using up the voices
around him.

That boy was snapped in a glare
once that made both eyes
wink like asterisks, adding to the
growing list of the parts of me
that hid from cameras. No doubt
I joked for the photographer's sake
about the risks of overexposure.

Now twenty years forward I no longer
hold my breath for the perfect pose
or worry about wrinkles in the trousers
I failed to take to the cleaners. The eyes
seem to be in focus too. And I like
the way I grin without knowing why
when my wife asks me to hold still
and say cheese. It is compensation
for having to pose in difficult light.

Who, after all, could have detected
the half of me that couldn't wait
to be developed, the dazzle in every
snapshot that couldn't be explained?
Now molecules scramble to take
a familiar shape at my side. In
the form I know best as my son
he crowds before the camera, refusing
to be left out of the one picture
where all of him can stand in
stripes, smiling.

JAMES B. JOHNSTON

The Photograph

From an envelope in her handbag,
She removed, with care,
The browned, black and white
She had preserved for over fifty years.
She remembered the day her sister left,
How she clung to her mother's skirts.
She remembered the day the photo arrived,
The tears as they gazed at the simple grave,
The handwritten inscription,
            Newmarket, Ontario.

It was the summer of 1976,
Mum's first visit to Canada.
The next Saturday,
As we set out on our search,
Mum told me about Mary.
She was seventeen
When she emigrated to the New World.
Sent to work in a sanatorium,
She contracted tuberculosis and
            Died, age twenty-one.

At the third and oldest cemetery,
The elderly keeper of graves
Brought us inside his small office.
As he opened the register of the dead,
We watched anxiously until
His unsteady finger stopped at
            McIlwain, Mary.

The old man led us in silence to the grave.
Mum placed fresh flowers by the headstone.
We took new photographs in color, but
As we left the cemetery,
Mum carefully placed the old black and white
In her purse, an unwritten epitaph,
            Gone but not forgotten.

LIBBA MOORE GRAY

Gene Crenshaw

Somewhere
among lettered stones
I search
for a brother I lost
and the small sister
he never knew.

My father carried him
in a white coffin
on the back seat of a Ford
to this Bedford cemetery.

He was a Depression baby
died too soon, the cord around his neck
they meant to mark his grave
but money was lean that year.

"This is your brother," they said.

"Remember."

and I looked
and was afraid
What did I know of death
or the manchild
my father needed?

I stooped and picked clover
to string bracelets for my wrists.
They yanked my hair.

"Be still child
Can't you ever be still?"

I wet myself—
My socks stuck to my legs

dried yellow in my shoes
I was still

They handed me to Willie Rudd
who held me close
folded my embarrassment
in her large lap.

I was hushed by her voice
the smell of her blackness
against my face

and the child was buried

now with the wind stirring the clover
the powdered bones rest
in some hollow sinking
under a chinaberry tree.

JANE CALFEE

Epitaph

But she was born for this:
To carry heat long past its appropriate time
Into January when the sun shrouded in dirty gauze
Made its own flimsy effort to prevail.
And cold men came to rest for awhile
On winter nights when breath and words both
Dissolve into the same ghostly mist and
Fail before the fire that, alone, insists.
Every charged moment becomes the memory of
A charged moment and those memories
Lock their hot talons then close.
The loss of summer is mean
To leaves and mad women
Who seem always to die
Of their own rich color.

II

Deep Wooded Ways

KATHERINE SMITH

Fall Topics

Let's talk about pumpkins,
red leaves, fires. Melons
fantastically designed
to match what happens
when you kiss me. Let's

discuss how the bees
come to blue cornflowers
at the end of summer
without a word, how

inside tiger lilies and tulips
is a light, a line of thought
that ascends, that ends
when you hear me. Let's

talk about the nine planets,
how the weight of them on us
isn't so heavy to bear. How
the sun, a star, loves water,

goes down over the ocean
like thistles set into
a vase, like a face
thinking up the real world
of gnats and grass, corn

and wheat. The harmony
is autumn. The secret
is winter. Let's talk
about red leaves.

First Place
Libba Moore Gray Poetry Prize

43

DANIEL ROOP

Opening

> I live my life in growing orbits.
> —Rainer Maria Rilke

Raise your hand to cover a section of sky. Half of the pinpricks
   you obscure are stars, the rest complete galaxies.
The world envisioned as a bowling ball is flat enough to bowl strikes,
   Everest only the height of a single sheaf of paper.
This, quite simply, makes me feel small. Here, on my back in the yard
   I have known my entire life, I think about the deception of endings.
This is grass. It is green. This is one red ant. This is my arm.
   This is soil. This is my pad, and pen.
I draw these lines around my life as we all do, searching for good
   figure by laws bred into me: nearness, continuity, similarity.

Take your hand down, now. Let each finger fall as unity joins
   your flesh, into arm, into pen, into song.
Tomorrow I will follow the roads to the library and open a book,
   which flows into table, to floor, earth, galaxy.
I will find a photograph of the corner of the universe where I want
   to be, and perhaps I will go there, perhaps I will stay.
The only answer is to love everything, to hold figure and ground
   as part of yourself, to embrace it all, the only closure.

FLORENCE MCNABB

Mountain Song

We came down Mt. LeConte in early
June all a-sog, the rain cool on our
noses, your steps spongy behind mine,

no snap of twigs just the mush,
mush of leaves and earth. Even
the edges of stones felt soft and

beamed their wetness. Our words
hung in bubbles, lingering above
us in the silent mist. We spoke

of streams switching away from us
then back again as we wound around
the mountain faces; a red-cheeked

salamander, its tail crushed on a rock
by a Vibram-soled boot; a pool of rain-
drops lounging in a cobweb hammock;

a rufous-sided towhee calling us to
Drink your tea, drink your tea.
A junco followed us to a rock shelter

where you read to me of Huck Finn's
escape from his father, and we talked
about Huck, the river and the stars

and rafts he counted when he was lone-
some, and you said a body never had to
be lonely, seeing everything around you

and liking yourself. If there were no
endings, of trails or books or such,
if there were no bottoms of mountains,

we might still be descending LeConte,
and this would not be the first day
of summer for it would always be spring,

an early June day, our bodies glistening
with each other, with each other,
not with the rain, not with the rain.

HEATHER DOBBINS

Goodbye

for Melissa Range

You
        wear your hair down—
                wind-brushed bark strands,
veined wings of leaves rupture yellow
                    (as I will gray later),
leap from their summer lovers.
                Ah, we *are* transitory.
You, at least, exit in full radiance—
                gold, crimson,
orange smeared after
             autumn goodbyes:
My stem grasped, chlorophyll fiber
                after fiber locked
into you during wind
           We have kissed
throughout rain,
           interweaving a silk sky pilgrimage.
You abandon without struggle.
        This is the way love
           should be.
I braid my small body into you—
           become part of the changing temple.

ROSE BECALLO RANEY

Fresh

He stands by the wheelbarrow full of sweet potatoes.
"Big as your arm," he says, turning
tubers over in their dust and soft clods.

Fuzzy root hairs hang down from them—fresh, ripe,
snapping with harsh orange in brown dirt skins.
He scrubs them down, sloughs off warm mud,

gnarled fingers knuckling in the knots of his work
as he dreams the steaming baked potatoes
mashed across with butter, yellow running

with some of the white corn and those beefsteak
tomatoes: wavering rinds, sliced-through sleeves.
The smile wrinkles as his shirt billows soft.

CONNIE JORDAN GREEN

Psalm to the Earthworm

Regard the earthworm
who lives in soil,
who hungers and humps
and hollows and hallows,
who gives to soil his daily bread,

who greets water
as she journeys from sky to cave—
she who circles and clasps
and washes and wells,
she of gift or fury alike;

who knows wind by rumor—
wind of the far north
who freezes and heaves,
who sends the earthworm deep,
shining and slipping, a silent passage;

eyeless, earless,
less than snake or eel,
this tube of skin and mouth
who year after year
swallows the earth.

HELEN DIACOMICHAL TURLEY

Ground Water

It is still.

No. Ripples ride it when
there is a cataclysm above,
then deep below.

Finally, we see beginnings
of a surfacing, smiling spring
that makes our leapings last.

IRA HARRISON

I Like

I like the way you move—
Your sway

A little south of smooth,
Like the last lingering leaf
On a silver maple tree.

ART STEWART

Shouting Down the Water

Ice, sleet, harsh
edge of winter gives way to
snap and crack

of frost-heave,
birth-pang, roar of
thunder, Olé!

One crocus
creaks up out of the
hard rocks,

purple,
rising early, sweet tongue,
shouting down the water

50

CONNIE JORDAN GREEN

Song for the Cellar

Wine bottles have bedded down
in air dank and dark
in dust and debris where mice scurry
where crickets hatch and all that lacks light
that likes the furry dark,
the thick, the heavy
where dark knows nothing of bud
of planting, pruning,
of the bee's journey, the insect's hope,

the wine's own light growing within—
silent, still, born of vines,
of leaf and hill and sun and rain,
a beginning so bright
the dark works hard to conceal.

DORIS IVIE

On Contemplating Crop Circles

The last theory I read blamed them on hedgehogs.
      Obliged to repeat timeless ceremonies,
      thousands of breastplated hedgehogs gather and
      plod in file, pounding down circles as they weave their rites
          in fields they call their own at dusk.
      Blindly they beat out bands flanked by labyrinthine paths
          that point back to the inescapable center.
Hedgehogs! Devas! Plasma! Still the crop circle theories teem.

Yet this slow summer afternoon I am compelled to reflect
      on the wheat field that lay across the road from my childhood,
      the field where bashed-down whorls surfaced overnight
      as unexpectedly as the insistent desires
      that blossom from a child's unwary innocence.

That summer I asked a leather-skinned sharecropper
      who wore a hat found only in old paintings
      why he produced those strange designs:
      "Why do you mow in circles and then stop?"
      (blithely ignoring that the wheat was mashed, not mowed).

He lowered his eyes as if I had asked him
      why he spent so long in the bathroom.
      "I don't do nothin'. It just happens. Overnight."
      He caught my glance, then dropped his chin ten more degrees.

Still to this day I can picture him,
      staring dumbfoundedly at the ground, defeated by mystery.
Into that faded mind's eye vision wafts an image of Millet.
Only Dali's x-ray eyes could discern the small, painted-out coffin
      the parents mourned as they bowed for Angelus.

Today my suburban lawn presents no such mysteries.
      Instead, I ponder questions of too-early death,
      unwarranted suffering, and the ugliness
      that compounds the insults of age.
Maybe that is why I revert to contemplating crop circles.
Perhaps before the earth turns bare some renegade restorer
      will plumb *Columbus Discovering the New World*
      and unsheathe the secret of their source.

51

JULIANA GRAY

Crossing

I see their dark eyes pass over me, perfectly round,
impenetrable. This is our arrangement. I see them now
as I never did then, taking shape in the brush near
the edge of the highway. Their haunches bulged into
gorgeous knots, their necks curved down with intent.
When I was eight years old and riding with my family
in south Alabama, six deer magically emerged from the woods
and leaped over our car. The last one's hoof left
a starburst in my window as it leaped. I never saw
them coming, only their flashing tails as they bounded
into the grass on the other side. Strange, then,
that they are so clear to me now. As if to compensate
for my head being turned in the wrong direction
those years ago, they appear to me now behind closed eyes:
smooth flanks, velveted antlers, walking towards me
on bronze hooves almost too delicate to support them.
Their black eyes look into mine and tell me the meanings
of grace, and of benediction in its subtlest forms.

DOROTHY FOLTZ-GRAY

Caterpillars

They remind me of punishment,
of my mother's broken yardstick,
its dead arm folding toward me.
This is where I slipped:
on the wet, green slope,
where the grass bruises,
and the black dirt shines
like the polish of a fresh shin cut.
Nearby, lilacs hang and grass
surrounds fallen crabapples.
Above the stone walk, caterpillars
weave nets they cling to. My mother
bends over me. Her bright red mouth
grips the unbreakable air.

DAVID HUNTER

Words Have Teeth

Words have teeth.
Already
I've lost three fingers
And now feel
A gnawing sensation
Where the ankle bones join.
Two fingers were lost to truth
And the other to a lie.
It does not matter, I suppose.
Words are words
And the deer never asks
The species
Of the predator that devours it.

BILL BROWN

"A Night of Yelling Couldn't Coax Cows Out of Deadly Barn"
—Cooperstown News Bureau, Middleburgh, NY, 2-2-96

Schoharie Creek couldn't hold.
Four feet of snow melted in as many hours.
Riffles turned to cascades, cross logs to weirs.
A churning damnation of red clay
burst out of its banks.

It was the ark gone wrong,
puppies floating, calves knee deep
in wet straw. Then it was waist deep;
he got what he could to the loft,
nine puppies, eight calves, the dog.

The horses knew enough to run
for higher ground, but cows,
right for milking, scared dumb,
stayed where they thought safety was.

He sang to them all night,
calling each cow by name,
to let a voice they trusted
startle them past drowning, hypothermia.
There were curses late when his herd
was dying, a horror of white eyes
shaking a wooden cavern to blindness;
and all that goddamned bellowing, gurgling,
"Sweet Jesus, save my heart from this."

Sixty-nine milkers and calves dead in the morning,
a few survivors stood on their bodies.
But a sanity shared by the tenderness of puppies,
the hunger of calves kept his hands busy,
a mercy denied Job.

ELIZABETH HOWARD

Waiting

Honey, you just go right ahead
and ask him all the questions you like.
He ain't busy. He ain't doing nothing
but setting in the porch rocker.
He don't need a case manager for that.
He ain't got much of a case
to manage now anyhow.
I tell you when he needed you—
when our son was killed in the war.
We both needed a case manager then.
And he could a used you the time
the staple gun shot a hole in his side,
and he was laid up for weeks
with a rot in the guts.
He could a used you right often
during the forty years he worked
his tail off in that stingy plant.
But the times he couldn't work
was the worst. When he was laid off,
or when there was union talk
and the big-Ike managers shut
the plant down just for spite.
You should a been here them days—
when we didn't have nothing to eat
but weevily beans and shriveled potatoes.
All them years, he dreamed of the creekbank,
willow shade, and bluegill,
but now that time hangs over his head
like a cloud of toxic waste,
he's too woreout to dig worms
and bait the hook.
He just sets there with his arms
folded, waiting to die.

55

SUE RICHARDSON ORR

Woods Away

Men in hardhats come
to bludgeon a road through the woods
with tree cutters, tree eaters, tree haulers.

They leave rows of birch
just next to the water to hide the ravage
but, through the leaves, I can see the yellow Cat.

Up front tree cutters
beaver through forests of green-topped giants.
I watch sky branches quake, shake, disappear.

Tree eaters bite down
around the trunks and pull their feet free,
like dinosaurs plucking lunch from a burrow hole.

The tree haulers come
in many-wheeled trucks with big open beds and wait
for the gyro man to puppeteer his rig their way.

Roots, trunks, limbs, bodies
are stuffed into the metal mouth, tasted,
then spit out, as if they had gone bad, into piles.

Truck hearses roll out...
hauling corpses of the forest to a grave
somewhere away from the place that grew them tall.

PAT BENJAMIN

Myrtle Warbler

So small a thing
to turn the day around
and point it towards
the sun!

Only a tiny ball
of bones and feathers
black and white and gold
and yet those tiny wands
can brush away
the nightmare mists
of early morning dreams,

the fogs I go lurching
through   alone and lost
like Holmes on the wild
moors   pursued by the
savage Hound
but not so clever as he.
I am unable to
track down, subdue my foe.

Instead, I hide
in the nearest thicket
and watch
for a small bird.

LEAH PREWITT

Bumper

Harvey bumps
His ninety-five pounds
Of muscle and fur through the world.

He is seven years old now;
There is arthritis in his
Right hind leg.
But it rarely stops him
From bumping up on the bed
At first light,
Vaulting over me,
Then whooshing down,
His head nestling
In the cradle of my waist.

When he's frisky, he snurfs
And slurfs, rubbing his head
Against me, against the bed,
Eyes imploring me to bump back
Until we wrestle
Like teenagers in
An imaginary pillow fight.

He doesn't always know where
His body is.
He crashes into me,
Clipping me off at the knees;
I never have penalty flags
In my pocket
At the right moment.

When I cry in the lonely night
Harvey bumps my hands,
Wanting to push my heart
Into a better path
Where everything

Is a morning in bed
With things that bump
In the light.

ROBERT CUMMING

She Dreams

A muffled growl, a soft staccato bark—
a fitful forefoot paws the languid air.
"She dreams," I said. "She penetrates the dark
recesses of some murky stygian lair."
I also dream, but not of cats who dare
to infiltrate our designated space.
I dream of rugged autumn trails where
we struggled through the tangled forest lace.
She moves with such intensity and grace,
a proper part of nature so it seems,
that we expect, and see, a focused face
of ardent wakefulness; and yet she dreams!
Through wind, rain, fleas, and frequent scenes of strife
we dreamers share a buoyant view of life.

MARILYN KALLET

December Journal

Grey and grey
    and the heart grows afraid
too many branches point downward
    phalanges of grey   switches
the witch's spell shoots
    forth more cold, banishing birds
nothing for the eye—

Now that the herd
    has been sold
oats along the roadside
    grow thick and high
pale silk brushes
    under last night's moon
sadness in such luxury
    uneaten
allowed to swell like an ocean

On the pasture road
    Anna in her red coat walks
deep in meditation   red earmuffs
    what music gathers her in?
Her white hair disappears
    past the tangles of brown boxwood.
The winter sun this morning
    not as bright as her hair
whiter than the memory
    of whiteness.

    Amazing!
A cardinal glows brighter
    amid brown branches,
Suddenly three red
    bellies round like fruit
but weightless, take flight
    all flight

as if arriving when called for
an answer
on twigs too delicate
to hold anything but air

Hold still—
a flock of them!
Fifty maybe? walking
shining through brown
tangled branches
who no longer believes in
birdsign? Beauty
its own fortune
black beaks pecking the ground

Why not live outside the self?
hopping up branches like stairs
flying through tangled brush

Unscathed by briars
these will get through
to wake the world

Gone now
to the far trees
small as insects
did I imagine flight?

Red against grey
dazzling moments
swoop past—

Look! you tell yourself
as a mother might instruct a child
this is our world
isn't it ravishing?

CONNIE JORDAN GREEN

Laying a Fire

Come at laying fire with skill
developed through long years of knowing wood.

In early afternoon, while the sun still shines,
think of fire. Gather twigs, sticks—
dry bits that'll catch a flame and hold it
for logs to ignite.

Pile tinder abundantly on the cold hearth—
pine needles, burnished and brown,
leathered leaves or crumpled papers
eager for fire. Above them stack cross-hatch

kindling you've gathered in sunlight.
Finally, logs you laid by last winter,
logs that have seasoned and dried
readying themselves for flame. Tepee the logs

leaning them together so flames rise
through the center, heat caught to kindle.
A generous hand keeps fire burning all night,
darkness and cold hanging beyond the walls

as forgotten as the labor of chopping and gathering,
all now become flame,
yellow, orange, blue, and white—
the earnest heat rising from your skill.

DANIEL ROOP

Clearing

Listen: See if you can hear what I cannot.
See if you can find the voice
that called me back here, to the woods
across from my childhood home, the boundless place
we escaped to when limits took form around us.
This is lush for miles, greenery beaded heavy
with July heat. I stand in the road for hours
as the sun beats down, scared to enter
until nightfall. Leaves lie across me like palms,
promising to heal one last time, as I step in slowly.
I find the old trails with great effort, thorns tearing flesh
like paper; I am the vine they grew from. I am home,
in the center, the fort we never finished building.
There are still loose boards here, saturated with rain,
blanketed with thick brown mushrooms. This world
has no time for nostalgia.

I kneel down, plant my hands in the soil,
and pull up rich black earth, nails and glass,
rusted bottle caps. I rose from this. It sifts
through my fingers' small town slowly. I stand up
and my knees pop loud and quick like decades.
Energy is finite; I cannot leave yet. Familiar sounds
surround me, blending into each other. Listen: If you find
the answer, do not tell me. This is about the process.

Sharp branches rip my shirt, scrape skin from my back,
pores taste the blood that fuels them. Through these trees,
one star shines—I trace it for future reference. One moment
later I lose it, my throat opens to surrender. Before it can,
I fill it with dirt, swallow mouthfuls until I collapse. I lie on my back
in the clearing, belly swollen full of steaming earth. A crow
calls above. I isolate the sound. Worms work underneath,
each one finding a sympathetic nerve in me. Near morning,
I belch hot stones, search them for messages under light
from dead stars that still burn. Nothing yet. No matter.
The same sun rises: I am here. I am asking.

EDWARD FRANCISCO

Mowing

Always some doubt about it starting.
The old mower coughs a syllable, then
fires to life before the startled landscape.
No country club green here, I set
the blades high enough to roll over
my barely cultivated rural lawn—once
rocky farm land, then a pasture, now
my yard bumped with the skulls of rocks
never buried far beneath the soil.
It is mildly threatening terrain for having
been neglected a week longer than I
intended. I scarcely know what I'll find
once I start to lay the grass in swales.

I attack at once, no sweeter pleasure
than mowing down the American landscape.
I watch as grass fans out from the gills
of the mower that blindly knows its
direction of intersecting lines and soft
right angles, veering only for stumps
and the odd tangle of roots resisting
easy identification. Not so other patches
where I wade in the lithesome plantain
or whack at irritable poison ivy
or stop to pluck some wild marbled strawberries.
Special fun up ahead: a plantation of
worker ants never expecting the great
sucking tornado that leaves the little boogers
staggering in chaos.

In fact, crawlers of all shapes and
persuasions line up along a yardstick
of color dissolving into a single
shade of green thought, getting lost now
in quick-bitten curves that strain and
collapse in a jittery treble clef of

broken motion. Quick shift: I'd help
them to safety if I could, but no
time now, no time for any but an
abrupt toad squinting as if measuring
the driveway's height he scales before
thumping to safety. We have made a
good job of it and can even stop to rest
now, if only for a while to sniff
the broken-headed mint fragrant as
last night's thought of standing in
the cool-footed grass.

EARLINE McCLAIN

Moon Morn

Lookit that rag-tag moon
Litterin' the morning sky!
Look lak some messed over, mos' gone cream pie
Maybe the morning broke too soon
'Fore you'd said goodbye.
But your time's done come and gone.
You've lingered 'round just a bit too long.
You've gotta give way to a greater light.
It's not your day,
Your province is night.
Git yosef outta sight!
You can come on back when the sun's at rest
And the sky's not so blue,
But right now you're a raggedy mess!
Goodbye! Be off with you.

WILLIAM H. P. NEVILS

Exorcism

Fat crows nag and caw, big as hens
and black as evil where they gather.
I watch them gather at The Feast of Seeds
after the mowing, fence-row thugs,
freshly fouled from a roadside kill.
Blacker one after blacker one they come,
and sicken, like the smell
of fresh blood and bad whiskey.
Begone, you who desecrate my door!
All of you: Now! Begone!
who take in vain
the noon-flood's name!

DORIS GOVE

Six Rides at the Green Meadow Amusement Park

The first is a jumping spider. Gripping tufts of fur, we fly
up and up, past the grass tops, trailing silk.
Then, with a noiseless pounce, we land
beside a crystal globe, a dewdrop.
Eight legs spring as one and we rise to a flower face.
Then, with silent screams, we plunge into shadow, under last year's leaves.

For the next ride, we go to the water. One mosquito leaves
as we board the next. A fly
fastens our seatbelts, and we face
the sun. The two filmy wings purr like silk,
lifting us high above the meadow. Then we drop,
buzz 'round the blood-pulsing naked ear of a rabbit, and land.

On the next ride, we glide closer to the land.
We float on soft slime among the leaves,
reclining on a slug's back. We hear a daisy petal drop
and watch an acorn sprout, as others fly

past our sweet, sinuous river of silk.
The slug glances left and right, inner peace glowing on its face.

Next ride, we are just barely on, and the wind's in our face.
The centipede's needle feet clatter across the land
hurtling us over, under, around, through, between. Strands of spider silk
slap across our eyes, and the bottoms of nettle leaves
burn bare legs and shoulders. We cling, we fly.
We swerve, veer, crash, spin, tumble, lurch, and finally, we let go and drop.

The next ride stands at first, chewing on a single drop
of nectar. Then she sticks her furry face
into a wax cell and spits fresh honey. We fly
straight out of the hive, 7 degrees north-by-northwest, 121.53 meters, to land
on a head of white clover. Our bee leaves
no petal unturned, and heads home, detouring only for an orb of deadly silk.

The last, the bagworm caterpillar funhouse, has a door of silk.
We crawl in, brushing unknowns from our hair, and drop
in darkness on a woven slide of stems and leaves.
We plop into a marshmallow monster with no face
who dangles from a twig and never touches land,
never crawls, never hides, never wanders and, if female, will never even fly.

The shadows from the leaves grow long. It's time to face
the journey home. But as we cross the meadow land,
and feel the misty silk strands drop away, we long again to fly.

LINDA SCHAIBLE

The Red Light Café

for Caroline and Page

They were both singing, the mother
mouthing the words, while the daughter
was open-throated and full,

out above the noise
that takes a bar into sunrise.
Birds are gone that way:

a thrashing of feathers from the limbs
of an oak, then the wild song.
I have spent days on a porch

watching crows overtake the yard,
their shadows running over the grass,
the living transformed by earth and passing light.

They are not the bird, but the thing that allows
the bird to be the bird:
not the bones and feathers

that scatter across the earth,
but a brilliance of noise gathered in by darkness.

KATHERINE SMITH

Lullaby

After the storm
the field mouse

has no home,
no redemption.

Stillness is
his only lullaby.

●

There's little comfort
in truth,

flushed from
a thicket, soft

brown birds
scattering in every

direction
except the one

taken by
the bullet. The

birds
fly on, not

caring how
still the grass is

now, how
full of grace.

●

The pasture is something
to believe in, lucidity

of long grass and wind
in which lovers sleep

touching so
lightly

that sleep
which assumes grief.

●

Light moves
from body to body,

yellow finch
flirting with

fence posts,
a song

of few
syllables

that says there
will never be

enough time
to find out

what truth is. And
so we sleep.

ELIZABETH HOWARD

First Frost

The chrysanthemums along the rock wall
are blooming at last—white and gold and purple.
But down in the hollow where the woods
are heady with cricket song and pine scent,
I hear katydids calling long before sundown.
Gonna frost! Gonna frost!
Soon, my pretty flowers will all be gone.
Just thinking about it gets me down.
I fill my towsack with hickories, stopping
to savor the chorus of cricket and katydid,
for it will vanish with my flowers.

As I climb the hill to the house,
a great red-headed bird swoops over, squawking,
lights in the giant oak with the hollow heart.
A wood Kate, in a halo of scarlet leaves.
My spirits soar at the sight.

I pick a fruitjar full of chrysanthemums,
set them on the table where the sun streams in,
start cracking hickories, and making plans.
The persimmons on the hillside
are the plumpest I've seen in years.
After the frost, they'll ripen in a hurry.
While that woodpecker's eating my suet,
I'll have persimmon wine and hickory-nut cake.

BRIAN GRIFFIN

On Reading the Autobiography of Nelson Mandela

They made a stone of you, shaker of trees:
chiselled you sharp and clear
to set time still and hide you
from our sight, for future eyes.

Like elders on some courthouse lawn,
they buried you, time capsule:
their gold shovels, our applause,
this severed bit of Qunu
seeding the soil of Robben Island.

How many of these capsules
never meet some future light?
How often have we banished
what we treasure, love and fear?
How often have we smothered what we live for?

Even treasured bits of every day, of comfort and largesse
(coffined away for children's eyes to marvel and adore)
leave memory and moulder
like some tuber axed away
from the green and the gold
of tired leaves
and straining, hoarded sun.

We made a book of you, persistent root.
We never saw that time can stand so still
and then be right here with us, even now.

JANE CALFEE

Anniversary

We could be pioneers even in this
Overripe suburb whose borders buzz
With wasps, could fling back wet and
Laughing heads as we bend
Toward our own good work at
Separate ends of the same garden.

What more than this—to sit
And sweat in summer dirt, tending
Plump fruit as we ride the spinning
Earth, its full and deepening lap

And suffer again the trees their
Bright annual death, murmuring assent
Under a familiar sky
Grown thick with ages past heat
But somewhere cradling
The infant ions of summer once again.

ELIZABETH HOWARD

Thirst

From deep within the bedrock under my feet,
the thirst comes, and I have to go
across the miles to the valley
where tatters of my root tendrils are imprinted
like fossils of fiddlehead fern in ancient rock.
Where the spring bubbles
from the cave's hollow mouth,
I find the cup you left for me
hanging on the cedar stob.
I dip the earthy water and drink deep
of the light in the forest.
It sifts through the trees,
illuminating the white spill of wild strawberries;
indigo buntings, chattering like fairy
children, splash in the rippling water;
a pale crawfish, as dainty
as a dogwood petal,
scuttles from stone to stone;
a redbud stands at the head of the swale,
pink blossoms glowing softly.
I drink it all, the water sweet
as milk and honey.
But dark hawks soar across the valley,
eclipsing the light,
and I recall the Judas legend—
betrayal and anguish.
Over all, an oak limb, broken
in a winter storm, casts
the shadow of a cross, and I taste
the bitterness in the bottom of the cup.

LINDA PARSONS

The Master Teacher Holds His Class

for Jeff Daniel Marion

Think long, let the root of it work
down to your tailbone, stretch out
in your knees. Let the words sift
through gravel, bottlecaps, nails.
Let them simmer before they're born.

Scoop dirt from the riverbank, sniff it
for signs of rain, raise your fist
to the sun. Your blood beating in time
with noon, that old flow in your hand,
will lift your heavy heart off the ground.

Now stand in your own backyard,
tell your feet to breathe. Close the gate
a while, open it a while. Remember your
school days, your father's last days.
Wait for the night heron to show you his nest
and fold you in his black-eyed song.

Go into the forest and weep with the cherry.
Circle it like a baby's curl, run like sap
in its veins. Weep till you sway in its tune.
Reach till you know its deep, wooded ways.

Love many women, but settle on one
whose steppingstones lead to embrace,
who loves your smell more than cake.
Love the one who prepares herself
with lavender, who sends you to the clouds.

When you have fought the wind
for your wings, when you have come this far
and thought this long, when the root of it
has wound a path to the bone, you can walk
beside me and think a little longer.

BILL BROWN

Backwoods Vespers

The February evening snow whispers
through the stark of winter trees, masks
the upper bark of limbs, and hums a vespers
to a night so quiet, my heretic arms fumble the task
of bearing split oak to the kitchen hearth.
At mid-winter this act has become a litany
of wood to stove and the responding warmth,
a ritual which most nights brings me sanity.
After a day of teaching English in the city,
I relearn the ache of our little planet tilting
painfully back toward summer. I learn that pity
and fear are not just tragic words lilted
from a teacher's tired voice, and in the harsh night air
between hardwood and dumb sky, the mum necessity of prayer.

Honorable Mention
Libba Moore Gray Poetry Prize

III

Come Down to Earth

JEFF DANIEL MARION

Midway in His Life
on the Day After Failing
to Receive His Appointment
from the Emperor,
the Chinese Poet Reconsiders
the World

Beside my doorway this morning
the Lenten rose nods,
its bloom a blush of color
on yesterday's pale cheeks of snow.

Last night the faithful stars
appeared, steady travelers swinging their lanterns
through millions of dutiful rounds.
Who am I to them,
my days but a flintspark?

Now the old dog nuzzles my palm.
To her I am no title, not even a name,
just a friendly hand to scratch her belly,
to deliver her daily lump
of meat in a blue granite bowl.
She sniffs my legs, loving the scent
of all the dusty trails I've wandered
to come home.

By the river the blue heron stands
and waits, poised in the long patience.
Here the world offers itself, wave after wave
of mountains washing across the miles.
Here the sparrow sings from the sycamore.
I lift my voice
and come down to earth
here.

LINDA PARSONS

So Far Afield

I am all apple tree,
you are all pine.
You part the red cedars
with your toes. I wave
my petals, throw fruit
at your feet. You rise
to the occasion. I swing,
like a chariot, low and sweet.

My invitations come out
with the hung moon:
Leave your slight sway
on the wind,
drop your coneflowers
longing to root
just this side of the fence.

I've come far afield, you say,
needling the sky. I've blown
on the pants legs of boys.
So toss your blond limbs a mile
past the fence, where my seeds
lie in wait in the shocks.

I shake loose the swifts,
offer ripe yellows, saying:
Take to the leafless sky
where branches pine
away for their mates.
Find the far field,
the lone stand of shocks,
where my love
lies now in wait.

DORIS IVIE

Courting Dance

It is a courting dance, this dialectic.
We tremble at the intensity,
We stumble in the glare of mirrored brilliance.

Mutually awed, our eyes widen in incredulity
At each answered phrase, each perfect rhyme,
Each measured metaphor, each salutation and response.
Tenuously stroking our instruments,
We share our songs.

The earth is allowing us again
To turn our hands to tilling talents,
And we are just saying grace
Without even thinking of words.

We drift in time toward monumental musings
On what is driving us wild in each other's words.

Robert Cumming

World Without Names

What is joy, and what is heaviness
if neither pierce the brittle land of dreams?
In a world without names
the sky is still the sky.

If neither pierce the brittle land of dreams
the quick realities are real still—
the sky is still the sky,
pain marches silent, nameless, through the night.

The quick realities are real still:
Beethoven's silent cell, awash with startling sound,
pain marching silent, nameless, through the night.
Unlabeled thoughts and feelings fade away.

Beethoven's silent cell, awash with startling sound,
Homer's endless darkness filled with light,
unlabeled thoughts and feelings fade away.
When dim remembered shadows jostled there for space

Homer's endless darkness filled with light.
What is joy, and what is heaviness
when dim remembered shadows jostle still for space
in a world without names?

DAVID BOOKER

On the Line

Sometimes I am a brickmason, my hands laying down the Great Wall.
"Keep the barbarians out," I mutter,
only to find they have circled 'round, like tanks through the Argonne,
leaving me on the Maginot Line, my niggardly guns pointing out not in,
their Mongol faces smiling from space and time,
their noses long like panzers' snouts, laughing like cannonfire at the line they
see. "It's not long enough," they shout. "Not long enough. There's a crack in
Berlin."

Berlin, Berliner, blurred line, break in the line where a snout poked through.

"She's on the line," my mother says, calling out to the sandbox where I've
recreated my line of defense.
"She just wants to feed me a line," I answer, surveying my redoubt from
above. With a chalk line I could make sure my walls were level.

On line, firing line, finish line, end of the line, line of sight.
I did not see the line coming.

A line is a metaphorical device, the imagination connecting two ideas.
"To be or not to be."

A line is a mathematical fiction, the imaginary connecting of two points.
To be and not to be.

The bottom line: credits minus debits equals the answer. Minus, a solitary line
shoving two numbers apart. Plus, two lines in perpendicular alliance trying to
form a union. Equals, two lines at rest, their work done.

Time line, deadline, credit line, "Don't cross the picket line."
Fishing line, realign, thin blue line, narrow line between life and death, right
and wrong.
"Line up on my side," the line-item veto, "The line forms to the rear, buddy,"
but never to the front because the front is the future and the future is made of
circles that ring out forever; the past is made of lines that grow long in your
face, broken circles laid flat by the sweep of the second hand across a clock's
face, stretched out by gravity until a line becomes a wall, one second at a time.

But within each line lives a band of gray, narrow as the spectrum of visible light in the line of electromagnetic radiation, but wide as the imagination connecting two points, two people, the promise and the reality, the past and the future.

My mother holds the phone out the door. I see the line of her aged arm, the curve of the cordless receiver tethered to a voice by radio waves, the line of the antenna, and the circle at the antenna's top.

I take the phone from her. I place it to my ear.

My soul is a Möbius loop of emotions, a line twisted into a crazy eight, forever going from and coming to where it started, always discovering there is only one side. Promise and reality become promise again, past and future become present and move on.

"Which side are you on?" is my opening in a long line of questions as I feel my back against Hadrian's Wall.

KATHERINE SMITH

ABC

The alphabet is equally soil and seawind,
twenty-six wings that twist and turn in the air
then take to the land that gives them back
to the small hands that hold them, mineral-like

inside the lead of new pencils, before dancing
onto the page for the child whose learning
takes wing back through history
into prehistory, folding the alphabet under

a bed of loam, to be nibbled by silent animals
whose hooves stomp the alphabet down
into the valley floor where I first learned
twenty-six things.

LESLIE LaCHANCE

Nota Bene

Your book of Shakespeare, the one you lent me,
smells like oil, spice, smoke
and I see you in your apartment reading letters
from the queen before leaving me alone with your marginalia
in the vague candlelit rooms of some glovemaker's son and,
oh, that view of the Thames.
I remember all I gave away before I left,
like the children, a boy and a boy, traded to Florentine gypsies
for the price of a fortune.
Now here's the detritus of your destiny:
old furniture and a broken mandolin.
In a mahogany chest I find the things of yours
I am supposed to wear, but only the love poems fit.

CANDANCE W. REAVES

Wallpaper Roses

I remember wallpaper roses
in the house on Laurel Avenue,
their beauty surviving
students and poets
itinerant workers
in the knitting mills
down the road.

It was a good omen
to begin love in that room
with roses in bloom
tra la.

But the roses thereafter never opened,
never prospered,
withered,
sad heads hanging,
so I dried them
hoping to keep them longer.

Finally, the glass rose
from Tiffany
lasted the longest.
It's still in the china cabinet
on the shelf,
and where are you?
Making love in another house
with wallpaper roses watching?

BRAD VICE

Madrid

Death boarded the train in San Sebastian
and shadowed us all the way to Madrid.
From there the steel rail turned to bones.
We followed the femurs of horses
and other noble beasts into the city.
You glared out the window into the ancient sun.
You were happy to be home again
happy to exercise your tongue
in the martial language of your father,
the Colonel—dead now three years.
The skeletal porter fared thee well
and extended his palm for a gratuity.
Grim, I counted digits, converted dollars
to pesetas. His perpetual smile already
had me unnerved. Its lurid knowing curve
had the charm of a cut throat. Even
he knew we wouldn't be leaving together.
I remembered you went to visit your aunts—
those three shrouded sisters—misers of
virginity—quick with a hex, but good
cooks and good Catholics nevertheless.
I wonder do they still braid your hair
and prepare cockscomb soup for you
to drink. I stayed to wander the city hoping
you wouldn't miss the next train, the one I
vowed I'd be on. You did, but your father
was there waiting for me at the station,
in your drab olive dress decorated with
ribbons and medals. Tonight in the sleeper we
will make love and I will endure every sigh
of that militant tongue. Then just before
the train reaches Paris he will quietly
lead me by the hand into the hall
and shoot me for writing this poem.

Honorable Mention
Libba Moore Gray Poetry Prize

JAMES B. JOHNSTON

Exile

When advancing years slow my steps
And my mind turns increasingly
To the contemplation of past years,
Will I, in exile, fondly remember
The land of my birth? The land
I left when fear shrouded
The serenity of family life;
When bullets and bombs
Overshadowed the beauty of the mountains
And the music of the streams, and
My search for true freedom found fulfillment
In a new life in a strange land.

Will my recollections be of seashore walks
And Sunday outings, terraced houses
With their open-hearth warmth,
The milkman and his empties,
The pub and draft beer,
The charcoal-coated chimney sweep,
Brushes atop his shoulder?
Or will I only recall
Bricked-up houses and barbed-wire police stations,
Soldiers and searches, road ramps and rioting,
The deaths and division that made me leave
The island that was my home, the island
That is my home?

KAY NEWTON

The Marketplace in Old Algiers—1994

Just as the curfew lifts you slip out quietly,
trying not to wake the others. It's still dark
but a Turkish moon hangs low in the eastern sky
and the streets are filled with people who, like you,
pretend to ignore the corpse on the corner,
the smell of creosote from a school burning two blocks over.
You hope you've arrived at the market
in time to buy bread, milk, the basics.
You stand among women wrapped in black discretion;
pairs and pairs of dark eyes veiled with caution
glance furtively, avoiding more than a second's contact.
The long wait gives all of you what you least want:
time once again for your thoughts to circle
the endless path already covered far too often.
Around and around your mind goes,
a huge cat pacing a small cage.
All you want is to be free, but there's no way out.
Here you are, a refugee in your own homeland
where more than once you've said a sad goodbye
and left intending never to return.
Like an old sweetheart whose face
has grown hideous and unfamiliar
Algeria has called you back,
holds you once more in a stifling embrace
that squeezes the life out of hope, dreams, faith,
her fetid breath a poison gas that suffocates all longing.
Your outrage at her betrayal has long since worn down
to choked-back tears, a constant dull ache in the throat
fed by the memory of the love you once held for her.
The night retreats stealthily
as if driven back by the cry of the *muezzin.*
You pray by rote, devoid of all belief,
so filled is your heart with despair,
so intent your mind just to endure.
You count out your dwindling money with care,
gather your staples—even water is precious—

head back to your waiting family.
Through an open doorway a radio plays:
"Il n'y a pas d'amour heureux," intones the old chanteuse.
Amen, you think, *Amen.* The white light of another day
blinds you as you hurry on your way, a rat in a maze,
subject of some perverse experiment
conducted by a bored and wanton Being
to Whom your final outcome is a matter of minor significance.
And yet, and yet—when you reach your door
the baby's radiant smile, his arms spread wide in welcome:
a stirring reminder of why you keep on.
You know you will find a way out.

JENNY NASH

The Argument

You go, and before your foot leaves the stair,
to ward off the furious rush pouring
at me, I seize cold Chinese food, mooring
myself to it, beyond you and past care.
I eat neon green pods in ginger sauce
and dream of the almond gold waiter who
served me glances and soup, instead of you
as I dive into noodles like beige moss.

I feel better as monosodium
glutamate softens my senses and frees
my brain. I know how to weave long bamboo
shoots into a net, holding me safe from
hurt, and if I eat enough fortune cookies
I will become too fat and wise for you.

KATHERINE SMITH

Maritime

The body is
the rhythm

that pulls light down
to brush against

white ribs,
tiny fish

still illuminated
by the crest of the wave.

•

As if the tongue
were a tide

that could carry grief
far past the body,

the word
navigating

the reef
of terrible crystal,

small boat
that saves

the body from
its own beauty.

HELEN DIACOMICHAL TURLEY

Bony Fish

How does one turn down
little bony fish from the sea
surrounding Greece?

I take five and manage
to take the meat from three.

The other two are set aside
and looked at with equivalent
curious eye.

I'll have one more bite and
take a toothpick home with me

to remember Athens.

DEBBIE PATTON HOLLENBECK

My Anchor, My Love

Hold me gently in my place,
The place I choose myself.
Protect me from the cliffs,
Guard me from the shallows.
Do not keep me
When it is time to go.
Do not tangle
the lines I cannot see.

Hold me at arms' length
In the summer breeze.

Come with me
To sail the seas.

LESLIE LaCHANCE

Wishing We Had Seen Carmen *Out-of-Doors*

I blame Verona, where this sudden and unusual rain
left us with a good story, but no summer opera
in that old arena, a Roman holdout

where big Americans danced in their seats,
calling against the thunder for Carmen and her castanets,
deep in downpour denial, we read our soggy librettos
and knew she'd never show.

But we were losing things all along the way anyhow:
clothing, spare change, plane tickets, pictures,
what did it matter?

Still, I blame Verona, something about that sad
and wet defeat in an otherwise seeming season of triumph
rang more true.

It's one of those things you can't undo
or barely make better with telling,
like a lie.

It's one of those things you can't go back to,
wouldn't if you could, no matter what you say
you wanted.

LINDA LEE HARPER

What's to Come

May. And already 92°F
by one o'clock.
Ethel steams carrots,
her damp hair,
like a cheap wig,
curling at her cheeks.
The man love lends her
calls from upstairs,
an unheated voice shading
her resolution not to go to him.
He can be cruel unintentionally,
says her thighs are white
as chickens, not lilies,
her breasts small as young girls
who don't interest him,
her lambent hair, wild as spurge.
But his voice is always cool
as his hands when they read
the warm hills of her like a map,
a small continent shifting
as she unfolds under him,
his silky waters flooding
the stone of her heart.

JEFF CALLAHAN

Navigator

Beaumont smells like
motor oil and farts at two a.m.
Your father bites the tip off a Tampa Nugget
and spits out the window
as you cross another bridge.

This is Texas in the mid-sixties
and JFK is gone.
In the backseat your sister works
her mouth around a cookie
while your mother nods off,

her hair mashed flat against her hand.
Such a gathering of lights
along the river where the refineries
and pulp mills smolder
in their own stink.

It's your turn to hold the maps
and try to look important,
though you still don't know
where Beaumont is or why Corpus Christi
means *body of Christ.*

At ten you've just begun to feel
the sadness of adolescence,
as when one finally learns
to lie and pull it off
and so is sealed within the lie.

Is it that same loneliness
you feel now as you stare
at an empty ball field, its single tier
of bleachers ascending
like stairs into the dark?

You feel your eyes begin to close
as your father changes lanes,
the Impala lurching forward,
shoving you onward toward sleep
and whatever journey awaits you.

JOHN GROSS

Tennessee

A ten-klick walk, with hardly a halt
from the fire base at Gia Rhea.
Rinse the cup, then saddle up,
We've got to earn our pay.

An old rucksack slung on the back
is a home away from home.
A sterno stove in a bamboo grove,
no chance to eat alone.

The legs, they ache. The back, it breaks.
The monsoon's steamy hot.
Shift the gear, stifle the fear,
adjust the old steel pot.

A slap and a scratch, dig for a match
to burn a leech away.
Check the map, give it a tap.
That's far enough today.

Patrols are out, the colonel doubts
we'll get much rest tonight.
Mosquitoes drone and the troopers moan
as they dig in for the night.

The sunset's blaze through a humid haze
is all the eye can see.
With a rub of the eye, a blink and a sigh,
I long for Tennessee.

JOHN GROSS

Rotor-Wash Dancers

When a chopper landed, the kids came out
to dance in the rotor-wash wind.
They'd flap their arms and squeal and shout
and toss their heads and spin.

It was all brand new, this hurricane
that came from another world.
With palm leaves blowing, it watered their eyes
and made the red dust swirl.

When the big bird rose and dipped its nose,
and lifted up over the trees,
the dance slowed down and finally stopped,
and the revelers fell to their knees.

As palm fronds swayed and the whirlwind died,
they wiped the grit from their eyes.
Quiet once again, the heat returned,
and they hopefully looked to the skies.

LISA COFFMAN

The Boy with the Blueberries

Conceding the city hurt his simple head,
he goes home, into the blue mountains
that secure the horizon, and roll on,
side to side, touching, like a herd.

And he becomes cheap labor timbering
where woods lock darker onto what was town.
"That over there was the big garden" and so forth,
foundation showing like some lunar rim.

Beach slipped from the knife still smells like fish;
the mottled trail betrays the limping stag.
Houses close on the road in apparent watchfulness:
the clever ones plead to leave, then leave,

sometimes come back. Approaching them, he says,
failing to despise what will not have him,
"If you are here tomorrow I can bring berries.
I can find you all the berries you'd want."

"Thank you—we go today." As though they'd turned
after—what? some whistle, snatch of color
and stared and could not find it,
he leaves them wanting where they were not wanting.

MATT BROWN

leaving the south

this damn car never seems to work
he thinks
the man questions the vehicle's circulatory system
how such an intricate mesh of heated pipes
could become so familiar
to his calloused hands.

he slides out from under the thing
sweating
and wipes his brow
with an oily rag.

another man walks across the rooftops
leaving his black bootprints
in the melting tar
wearing a blue shirt and cap
a blue-collar santa of sorts

he has come to check
the ventilation fans
as the kitchen was getting hot.
the fans are frozen.
the rust is their aging
their motors never seem to work
he wipes them down
with an oily rag.

hearing noises in the kitchen
the woman hoists herself up
off the couch, the left cushion
much flatter than the others
the fried chicken seems to burn
itself off in the southern heat
but compensated by this evening's meal

having fried both legs and both wings
she wipes off the stove
with an oily rag.

this morning
as the fog burns itself off
in the southern heat
my body stretches its borders a little
my mind stretches its borders a little

my blue shirt no longer seems to fit
the southern heat.
I wipe off my brow
with my blue-collar rag
and walk away.

LIBBA MOORE GRAY

Being Home

I have a friend who said the mountains were oppressive
smothered her
any day   she said
green mold growing on her tongue
under her fingernails
moss for hair
green tendrils for arms and legs
she ran home to New Mexico
David left for San Antonio
Anne for Washington
Larry for Mississippi
Gretchen for South Carolina
Pat for Charlottesville
I'm still here
dipping green from mountain pools
blowing green smoke in the air
unwrapping kudzu vines from legs
listening to the whippoorwill sing a green hymn to the moon
while algae swims slowly over my lids.

Jesse Graves

New Year's Day

The sleepy men of my family linger
around the table to exchange stories—
snowstorms in Michigan
so cold the engine locked up,
the windshield frozen over
from the steam of your own breath.

Stories of driving at night
across the North Carolina border,
the hollow bottomless mouth of the Gorge
along the black edge of the road.
A bed of fog waiting, thick as cotton,
around curves so sharp all you could see
in the tilted side mirror
were the flickering lights
from brakes grinding to dust.

The men in my family are born exhausted,
smelling of diesel oil, carbon filters,
and gasoline,
our blood tainted in the womb
with chemicals we cannot pronounce.
They eat away at us until we are old,
but do not kill us, our veins
are thick, our hearts pump slowly.

101

RICHARD PATTON

Custodians

Future custodians of the planet
Fisher-Price shovels in hand,
Skip barefoot,
Following a trail of cigarette butts to a sandbox,
Squatting to excavate
Biggie Fries boxes while
Slicing their
Soles on
Broken bottles of beer.

Ann E. Thompson

Gone to Press

A nuts and bolts creature,
the German beast lies still
as men force feed her
cyan soy ink and oil her joints.
X-ray-like plates are fit
in her metal-fashioned belly,
and paper rolls are webbed
through her skeleton.
With the flick of switches,
power vibrates through her frame.
She churns with the clink
of parts moving in mechanic rhythm
as broadsheets snake
through her iron innards.
Black-handed old-timers
stand by as she stamps
on page after page,
bleeding the news
of Jack Owens, county sheriff,
who blew his head off
at the Gulf station
at Hollywood and James.
Old Ruff watches his child
spit the paper in his hand.
She will be tomorrow's dinosaur,
left to sit in the Smithsonian
and have her brittle bones
stared at by kids on field trips.

JAMES B. JOHNSTON

Stone Wall Fences

Rising a modest twenty-eight hundred feet above the sea,
The Mountains of Mourne are all the mountains to me.
How often their steep granite slopes have drawn me
From the confines of the city. How often, as children,
We followed the river Glen through Donard Forest.
Little we knew of oak and beech, elm and sycamore.
Our goal, to reach the open hillside, cross the stile and
Recapture our breath at the old icehouse on Thomas Mountain.

Today, again, we have left Belfast for the tranquility of the Mournes,
A Belfast bracing for bombs even as it gathers for peace.
Later, at three, we too will gather in the foothills of these mountains
To pursue the pollen of peace. This morning Slieve Donard
Is capped with a dusting of snow, but a welcome sun takes
The chill off a cold February morning as we rest alongside
The Mourne wall. I recall seeing an old stonemason maintain this wall.
Dressed in dungarees and wearing a duncher,
He set stone upon stone with roughened hands,
Building with care this wall of beauty and strength.

We are a land divided by stone wall fences and granite hearts.

We go on to the Silent Valley to experience, for a moment,
Complete stillness. This valley is an ocean apart from the bombs
That marked the ceasefire cessation. We want to tarry longer, but
Three o'clock approaches—as if our silent scream will be decisive
In restoring the ceasefire—two of ten thousand souls trying to
Make everything like it was just so, dismantling the walls of
Granite hearts, peace by piece.

DON SCALF

The Silos

Across the Clinch in early morn
The mark of day is always born
When sun and sky together meet
To link the two great silos.

Born two hundred years before,
The silos to my eyes afford
A grace, a single majesty
Of sentries on a shore.

In years of youth their bellies held
Silage from a farmer's dell,
But war between the North and South
Did turn their innards out.

In summer of 1862
The silos' walls saw gray and blue
And heard the roar of cannon mouth
But stood in double silence.

On afternoons in days of June,
Inside the dark and silent rooms
The soldiers laid their heads to cool,
Lost in sweet repose.

Winter's months brought many more,
Both men and boys, all battle torn
To warm their hands and fix their eyes
On fires within the walls.

Until the end of battle came
The humble silos' walls did claim
The weary men with faces blank
In search of sweet reprieve.

The years that followed that great war
Saw ivy creep from walls to shore
And inch its way from clay to top
And shroud the silos' walls.

The silos seem to be the same
But close inspection proves the claim
That 'neath the ivy's leaves is found
The truth the silos hold.

The silo on the left is said
To be of bricks as black as lead
With mortar 'tween the pitchy blocks
To seal its silence up.

The silo on the right is built
Of mudbricks cleanly parched of guilt;
The searing sun had baked them till
They shone of peerless white.

So seemingly they stand in two
And share a symmetry and hue
Of golden brown at sunset time,
Linked in lasting peace.

The ivy paints the silos' walls
In daylight, but when nighttime falls
The silos drape themselves in black,
No color can you tell.

In stinging silence darkness sinks
To show the world at morning's brink
That on the shore the silos stand
In muffled cry to man.

LINDA SCHAIBLE

Sheffield Steel

We are sitting in my mother's kitchen,
drinking coffee and talking about nothing.
She shows me a box of knives,
the long blades reflecting her face,
the pale colour of her eyes
not mine at all.

She begins to tell me her story,
and I drift past her. For me,
there is little of England in this house,
not even these knives look like
they have been through WWII, Sheffield Steel
engraved in a crest at the base of each blade.

On a shelf with the poems of Bishop and Owen,
is a hockey puck that is Canada for me;
it is a broken leg left to mend on its own,
bruising fights with French Canadians,
and a language I will never love.
How can this be the same as the knives:

my mother says "beautiful" and "pretty,"
while I say "bone-hard" and "black."

LINDA LEE HARPER

At the Butcher's

She loves the way he never hesitates,
lifts the steel shingle of meat cleaver high
past his head, then whacks the haunch or rib-boned
meat his other hand holds still as a dog
being groomed. He will ask what cuts she wants,
but like most June conversation about
weather, her answer never changes, week
after week the same thing. He wraps her cuts
in heavy paper as tenderly as
he might children in a blanket, stacks each
pack like folded flags, hands over the lot
to her, always careful to brush his thick
hand against her breast as he eases fresh
meat into her arms. She stands patiently,
every week, waiting, wondering how his
wife manages to scour his canvas
aprons white, how she deals with all that blood.

Honorable Mention
Libba Moore Gray Poetry Prize

ANGIE VICARS

Place Setting

I sit at the end
of her long wooden table
and sip my wine
from crystal I'm almost afraid to touch
I leave the silverware lying
in its solid silver state
it is too heavy for these hands of mine
I stare instead
at my polished reflection
the bones of my cheeks
in the bone of her china
this is a finer reflection
than I usually see
without a place setting of my own

108

JOAN SHROYER-KENO

The First Piece

She held the teaspoon at eye level.
Her strawberry blonde hair reflected
in the polished sterling as she felt
the cold weight of it on her fingertips.

In tiny flowers at the handle tip she saw
blossoms she would someday grow
at a home of her own. In its shiny shallow
bowl she saw a husband and then the children
she would one day feed with it.

When the salesman asked how many place
settings she would like today she said:
"One piece—this spoon."

JEREMIAH GREEN

A Quiet Meal

Beneath a streetlamp, a
    dark, empty parking lot washes
up,
    and crashes against
the curb.
The sidewalk
        snakes
                around the
restaurant, through
        pools of light
and craters of shadow.
Inside, the place is filled
    with warm light,
    the racket of cooking,
    quiet conversations,
    and warm food.
Come with me,
we can talk
    beneath the
country twang
    I'll buy you some
hashbrowns, chocolate pie,
    unlimited coffee refills—
they're comfort foods.
Relax, open up. We'll
    share each other's
closeness and warmth,
    pay the
                tab,
and go out
    together, into
        that
dark   night.

Honorable Mention
Young Writer's Prize

109

DAVID LAUVER

Nobody Does It Like ellA

She was built to last and had a streetwise face.
Time left some lines she didn't try to erase,
'Cause the years disappeared when she turned the lights down low.
At the bar she could mix any drink we could name,
She kept a good kitchen, but that's not why we came.
What she did after dinner's the reason we miss her so.

Her passion was music she'd share for a song,
The right mix of rhythms to keep us turned on.
All her sweet surprises left us longing for more.
She could belt out the blues or old-time rock 'n roll,
Cool jazz and hot country came from deep in her soul,
The only lines she drew were lines that she drew to her door.

Nobody does it like ellA used to
When she entertained for the fortunate few.
She made each night in the Old City new.
But now nobody does it like ellA,
Nobody does it like ellA Guru's.

ARTHUR SMITH

Chez Lucille

The truth is I'm wired
With you, music and talk
And me leaning close
To your hair
And your face
And that cruel place
In back of your ear
Where the skin's
Drawn over bone.

I'm all right, I couldn't be
Drunk enough
To not want you,
Not be taught
How that long and low,
That slow-rising
Note is best
Coaxed out of you.

The truth is
I hungered
For a woman onto whom
The primary colors could be
Pinwheeled,
And now it seems I had been
Hungering to prove
I was a fool.
Which I did and.
Did and.
Did.

Now I'm here with you, hearing
Jazz in that, loud jazz,
When it's late and I've been
Long alone.

ROSE BECALLO RANEY

Inmost Lyrics

When you come to me in the night
I will touch my lips to your shoulders;
I will hold you so,
a reveling cloud before thunder.

I know that I can say nothing
to show you this burgeoning love.
It draws me up
beyond the telephone wires.

I know that I can say nothing
on a morning after such dreams,
so singing inside,
I will take to the sky of this season.

I will take to the sweeping whiteness,
timeless, sunless and ashen—
this wordless sky,
pallid, pearly, and real.

JEFF DANIEL MARION

After Studying the Full Moon
Rising Over Snowy Fields
Beyond the River
Outside His Bedroom Window,
the Chinese Poet Dreams
of His Love Far Away

for Linda

No footprints to my doorway,
no trail coming home,
just this moon's light on snow
lying like silk, still and smooth
on the earth's skin.

What does the moon whisper
to the river in such light?

All the secrets of white—damask and linen,
bone china cups and lace curtains,
candles' warm glow on a table set for two?

I lie down on the pristine sheets
and remember peach blossoms fragrant
in spring, their perfume a hint
of you.

ARTHUR SMITH

The Rich Man Watches the Widower

He needs to touch her things,
The paper bags and ribbons,
The buttons and thread and small
Bright pieces of metal
That look like dainty rivets,
Though what a woman would need
Rivets for escapes him.

He carries them afterwards
Everywhere, coins
He shines by wearing them
Between his fingers when he's
Standing still and by being
The only one who can hear
Their currency when he walks.

JENNIFER VASIL

Ellington on 72

About ten miles outside Scottsboro
it starts to come in,
signal sticks on a scratch and then—
the slow rise of an alto or trumpet,
Ellington at 9:30 on Highway 72,
headlights' flash and groan of tires on asphalt.
I race toward style,
Exxons and resting semis blinking past,
the way I say, "Jazz these days
sounds like elevator music"
instead of neon behind glass,
energy that pricks hairs on my legs
at one note.

Nothing really to look at in the dark,
watch miles spin by on the odometer,
think too much in two seconds' delay
it takes to translate song lyrics to voice.
Johnny Hodges crawls between imagination
and glazed streetlights, the curve where the highway
changes from four-lane to backroad, squeezes
between bridge rails in high C then drops abrupt
to announcer's voice, South Pittsburgh, Tennessee.
It is late, and I'm halfway home.

DON SCALF

The Economics of Shine

The black boy slid his wooden box on the spit of Bourbon Street
And bet me my best dollar he knew where I got my feet;
I knew his game but pulled a buck and folded it real neat
Just to hear him say "You got 'em on the street, *tout de suite.*"

He knelt in the shade to shield his face and dug into his box
And pulled a can of Desert Tan, slapped it once and stopped,
Then flipped his fleece at both brogans to dust them like a mop
And slid a brush too gone for teeth along the sides and top.

He worked the weathered leather with his slickened fingertips,
And slapped the sides of both my feet and fixed them in his grip;
His grizzled head bobbed and weaved and sweat rolled off in drips
That spotted both tan shoetops black until he buffed them slick.

The wooden perch wobbled as he cobbled up the sides,
Then tapped a cadence with his toe and shouted dirty lies
At fools that passed and watched him work, imagining the sighs
They'd read back at the office in the office workers' eyes.

The Desert Tan took on a sheen and I had thought him done,
His face all slick from rubbing hard, his smile, once gone, had come
Again, but in his eyes I saw the fear that shine boys can't outrun,
That even when they've shined so well, the money doesn't come.

I paid him my best dollar, then a second dollar too
And watched him turn and scan the crowd to find another fool
To worship simple talent and to shield him in the cool
Of moneyed shadows overhead while he played by his rules.

Two minutes' work had yielded him two dollars, that's a switch
From the world of business deals where I'd always found my niche;
Then three men from out of town lined up to get their kicks,
And at sixty bucks an hour, they'd make this shine boy rich.

LESLIE LaCHANCE

Things They Could Say

They could say something like I know you have considered
the virtues of pure grain alcohol, but dismissed them all

Or, you would look perfect without hair, skin rubbed green
with french clay

They could say you smell like the desert like ice like snow, new
or old, like pond water like hay like babies' milk

They could say your smile reminds them of korean barbecue, red
peppers, rice and smoke

Of your voice they could say speak up and out like a giant
buddhist bell rung by monks on new year's eve

Your dancing, they could say, is queer, mindful of gravity though
deploying the laws of nature uncertainly

They could say your tongue reminds them of salsa

Your eyes of indigo tattoos

They could say let's go to cleveland, des moines, kalamazoo,
the hell with paris, forget rome

They could say tomorrow is another day to seize

And they could leave out the word love altogether

PAT BENJAMIN

Skyline Drive Motel

Last night, after the quarrel,
I secretly marveled
(in stony silence)
at the mountains' stony beauty,
their remote refusal to care.
I thought they would
surely stand
long after our small rockslide,
staunch in their solid glory.

As I closed my eyes,
sucking cold straws of comfort
to foster sleep,
I told myself, "Those mountains
will be here tomorrow,
fired by the morning sun."
But when morning came,
they were gone
and the whole green world
had died.

We two were still together,
but only a sea of mist
lapped at our door.
We had slept on the edge
of the breakers and somehow survived,
clinging, lashed tight
to our small rubber lifeboat.
It floats with the tide.
It bends; it is covered
with patches,
but still it survives.

GEORGE SCARBROUGH

I Think of Boxes from a Hospital Bed

for Bill Countess

When I was gangling
And growing tall,
I cached my pretties
In a hole in the wall.

When I was a young man,
One of four,
I got my half
Of a bureau drawer.

When I was a lover,
With fevers and poxes
I stacked my room
With darling boxes.

On floors and shelves,
On ledges and sills,
I heaped my containers,
From quilts to pills.

And though I pursued
My loves with vim,
There was at last
No room for them.

When matters came
To push and shove,
A house with storage
Was better than love.

Now my boxes and I
Are wrenched asunder
By various ills,
I lie and wonder,

When my stuff is put
In the best of them,
Who will inherit
The rest of them.

IV

The Work of the Living

LINDA LEE HARPER

Keats' Heart Wouldn't Burn

they say, calcified as his shin
which had the decency
to burn to ashes.

In Pizza Hut we ate salads
while they sewed Ben back up,
stapled him shut,
his heart newly corrected,
shunting blood the right direction
for the first time in eleven years,
and I wondered that if he died,
if we purified his bones in mortuary flames
would someone also find a heart
at the bottom of that kiln,
a sutured heart as cooked as ceramics,
white as china, small as a cup
you might hold in one hand?

ANN E. THOMPSON

Death of a Salesman

Creeping down the stairs,
I manage to press my weight
on each arthritic board.
I lean around the wall
to see the headphones
grip his ears like ticks.
The clock glares 5 a.m.
(alpha, mary).
In the craned lamp's spotlight,
he leans over the mic.
A thin string of smoke
unwinds from his Salem,
pinched between
the ashtray's grooves.
In an hour he will ease
the Buick out of the garage,
casting its headlights
over the rosebush's dew gems.
Pulling the curtain up,
he begins the play
where Willie left off,
only he peddles bricks
following Willie's ghost
into the white heart
of East Tennessee kilns.

LAUREL McNEELEY

Swallowing the Cancer

I didn't think of dying.
I thought of my fourth grade model of anatomy
bright and bold against the classroom,
the bruise of a heart
purpled with patches of tempera and brush,
cheap plastic kidneys,
chipped and yellowed as an old sunset photograph,
and simple privates displayed
with new, self-conscious names.
I became plastic that day,
I had never been so aware of body.
I pictured my serpent veins
twisting around the brittle synthetic,
shattering body,
the shards of my lungs floating in strange fluids.
My mind,
swallowed by its own faulty body of infection,
blemished and frayed,
is tired.
It is slow and sad like a voice,
weightless and lingering
from a throat of flour.

Honorable Mention
Libba Moore Gray Poetry Prize

EDYE ELLIS

Epitaph for a Late Bloomer

I didn't plan it this way.
I wanted to take more road trips
smell more fragrant blossoms
from my one successful attempt
at growing gardenias.
If things had been different,
I would have written a lot more poems,
tried harder to find that Carmen McRae album,
apologized once and to all
for all those wishy-washy
double messages.
I certainly would have had
more actual conversations
instead of all those
imaginary ones
and I would have sent those
endless letters I've been writing
in my head for years.
I would have done more things
that scared me
instead of spending
so much time avoiding them.
And, if I had known
I would meet you,
I would have made
almost any kind of bargain
for more time.

HELEN DIACOMICHAL TURLEY

The Winter View

Seems I viewed
you
in a winter
before
when icicles
strung themselves
around your cap
and only laughter
between us
made them fall.

It was in a dream,
but I cannot say
for sure
that the cap was
blue
like your blue eyes,
or green or gray,
like they are at times.

I wish I knew,
for then my pen could
write with certainty
and the search would
be no more.

The winter, nevertheless,
brings frozen faces
around us,
and I say the warmth
of ours
is to explore.

JENNIFER McKAIG

Blueberry Meditation

I searched through my purse for five minutes
looking for some matches
even though a lighter was in my pocket
because I wanted to see the spark
and be brought back
to that day when Jeremy taught me
how to light a match with one hand
and just maybe the spark
would bring him back just for a second
but it didn't
So I put my worn-out and worshipped
Paul Kenny tape in
and listened to his voice
weave in and out of my heartbeats and tears
and I could feel the wind that
swept me away in that great valley
and thought of those midnight skies
dusted with stars and fireflies
because he was that perfect crystal vase
that you wanted to touch
when you were little
because it was so pretty and shiny
but mom wouldn't let you
so all you could do was stand back and gaze
and hope that one day
you could be special enough and old enough
to caress it
And I thought of Jeremy again
and fingered the matches
that were now safe in my pocket
and closed my memories like a movie
on the back of my eyelids
and felt his shaking and scarred hand
grasping mine
as whispers of journeys
to the ends of moonlit trails

tickled my ear
and I felt his soft skin against my lips
wishing I could kiss the back of his neck
while he slept next to me
but the realization of the impossibility
made me leave my movie
and gaze blurrily upward
through the green velvet tapestry
of a big oak tree
where a single blue butterfly with silver
tipped wings flew from leaf to leaf
sprinkling fairy dust on my eyelashes
and I wanted to be that butterfly
because I could then float away
and meet my blue-eyed baby
by our crystal lake
and turn on the moon so that he would
not fear the darkness anymore
because he always brought me sunflowers
and security
when I most needed it
And I gave him incense that promised forever…and more
and shiny confetti hearts
to take the pain away
but the butterfly disappeared and took the
memories with it
And I lit another match to see the spark…
but it didn't.

Honorable Mention
Young Writer's Prize

CHARLOTTE PENCE

Common Infliction

Firecrackers explode above my brother's head,
crowning the football crowd with orange and white halos.
Everyone rises tightly at once
then spills over like a shaken can of soda pop,
in chants and shouts
pounding an earthquake into the stands.
But he never changes his stature,
The Thinker,
elbow resting on knee, face frowning in scrutiny.

I watch him with a full-turned stare,
scared by the pain I see there.
Watch his eyes riveted to the wet grass
he once cut his cleats through
after a life of training,
running at six,
despite the clouds of cold
puffed from his lips.

But he had a mishap.
Trust me, it was such a little one,
but on the wrong day.
So, he had a child four years later.
Displayed her on his forearm like a football and told me,
I just want to be comfortable now,
then pushed down her hurricane hair
licked hard by a cow.
We watched it spring up again.
I think that's when I vowed
to be weary of saying those words.

The rain falls in sharp drops around us
but he doesn't move.
Doesn't even shiver in the icy air
or ask the bored kid to stop kicking his kidney.
The fireworks explode again,

illuminating the sky,
corners of his eyes,
for just a second.
And I shudder.
at what
will be my lie.

DEBORAH SCAPEROTH

The Incantation

In the outer office,
the bald four-year-old
on her mother's lap
shares a fairytale book.
The child's eyes glow
against her ghostly pallor
as tales of gnomes and kings
fill her baby head.
I read my notes and see
her calmly waiting—as if her life,
an endless procession
of potions and spells,
weren't hanging in the balance.
Her mother turns the page; I flip her chart.
My throat tightens as I wish for
magic.
I call her name.

DOROTHY FOLTZ-GRAY

Revision

My mother rises out of a pool, her breasts so young
she smiles at the camera, at my father.
Pulling her body out of the water
into the air, he catches her and she smiles a second time.
Above her head the palm trees wave.
This is the night my father watches her walk down the steps
into the hotel lobby, and years later, when she is dying,
he remembers out loud this childless night
and the way men look at her.

BRAD VICE

Ontology

I am driving you to school.
It is cold and your lips are shivering blue
and I think I am waiting for a kiss.
I am telling you that Milton says angels understand
the universe as if it were a good line of poetry,
intuitive thought as opposed
to discursive.

The way I understood what the doctor
meant when he spoke of the spots on my back.
He said, *We are waiting for one*
to distinguish itself, as if they were students.
The mind lurches toward what the stomach
already knows.

You are preparing for a long life, happy enough
to let me ramble. God is static. I am telling you
God just is. To say that God is Love, or Light
or anything is just a metaphor.
I stop the car to let you out. I receive the long
awaited kiss. I am grateful.
You are grace.

The doctor was a professional.
He ran his finger down my back like a text
finding the odd errata of the flesh.
I think that everything we can know about God
lies on the surface.
On my tongue I'm tasting radium and cobalt,
those heavy metals.

JULIA BROWN

Scarlet Reminder

The coffee cup is stained with your bright smile.
I envy that it shared your crimson touch.
Beneath your lip print, Van Gogh's *Starry Night,*
its luster lost compared to lips as such.
The candle flickers like a firefly.
I blow it out. You're gone. What can I say?
The stars swirl on within the deep, blue sky.
I sigh and wipe the scarlet brand away.

EDYE ELLIS

Dog Days

Somewhere between
come here and get out
we find our places.
Somewhere between
terms of endearment
and grounds for dismissal
we find our spaces.
Somewhere between
the frown and the smile
we find traces
of our worth to you.
There is no road map.
We make our way
by the sound of your voice
and the animations of your face.
Somewhere between
approach and avoidance,
fear and risk,
history and herstory,
there is love.

LEAH PREWITT

This Table

The cabs stop near Peachtree
And we spill out like water moving
Downstream into the night.
I am caught up, a fish in this school
Moving with the others inside.

There is a crush in the bar
And someone buys me a drink.
When we start up to the restaurant
I remember that I have been here before.

The image of my sister follows me
Up the deep carpet on the wide stairs
To the softly lit room.
She has come to tend me in Atlanta.

This table is long and wide
And the cover is rich, sweeping
Down across my lap,
Draping me with soft cotton.

I am shifted onto the table,
My hands find the edges
Of the chilled metal just beyond my hips.

Around me the voices of my friends
Rise and fall
Against the backdrop of the waiters
Tending us with a splash of water
Into the glass at just the right moment,
Weaving among diners
And over the plush floor.

The room echoes.
They loom above me,
Put cold gel on my head,

On my chest,
On my legs,
Cover it with sticky pads
Attach me to electrodes.
There is already a tube
In my arm.
They note the time on the big clock;
The last thing I remember.

When the meal is finished
We push back the cherry chairs
And breathe deeply,
Contented with sipping sweet coffee,
Swirling fine French brandy.
We bask in our filled bellies.

I wake in a fog of morphine
The sheets surround me
Crisp and white
Even the smell is stiff.
My left breast is lost,
Forever, and I am numb.

You reach for my hand,
Seeing my eyes fill, and
I tell you, whispering,
What was done to me
The last time I left here,
What awaited me in the morning.

In the taxi you tell me,
"You will go home this night;
In the den that is our bed
I will lick your scars
Until you fall into sleep,
Waking with the soft light,
Safe in my arms."

MARILYN KALLET

The Only Way

for May Sarton, 1912-1995

Pale wheat before the black mountain
a quick flock of wrens—
I meet you again in a house of gathering.

The lights are on, May,
the pines greener in winter light.
I come to you alone, the only way.

The busy world falls away
in the presence of mountains.
The world stripped down for light.

How long it has taken me
to say goodbye! You were not easy.
Your words scalded me.

When love's gone I need you most.
You always met me there—
raged at anyone who hurt me.

In my grief, you were mine.
Now you are loss too.
The light goes, the branches darken.

Stay with me awhile
in the low sky and mountains.
Wrens rest in the boxwood.

Then they are simply not there.
Absence and presence
fixed lightly to their wings.

LISA COFFMAN

Courage, or
One of Gene Horner's Fiddles

After I write *My face burned and I wanted to cry*
I watch Kathleen Osborne, who was on oxygen all winter,
walk slowly by the canal, with the jerking motions of a small boat
when the people in it move or change places on their knees.
You don't know nothing. Do you? Gene had said.
I had come to see about buying a fiddle.
Rainy day, the Cumberlands blunting any notion of future.
Well, I said. My face burned and I wanted to cry.
Then he played for me, he would have played for anyone,
a dark maple fiddle he'd made, such a pure sound
it could have belonged to either of us,
it seemed to rise from the frets of my wrists, my curled hands.
We are wrong about courage. It is closer to music.
It rises from us simply as we move in this life, or submit.

LIBBA MOORE GRAY

Dancing

If you know the music
of this planet
please will you play it now for me?
Once I danced on mountains
and moved so fast
tree leaves laced with sunlight
dazzled me.
My feet swirled pine needles into whirlwinds,
circled the spotted doe,
leaped the wild stag,
made shadows
as if the feet were wings of white feathers.
And I danced by the sea
where waves lulled me
like my mother when I slept beneath her heart.
And I danced on rooftops until tiles trembled
like a thousand wind chimes before a summer storm.

I am so still now
and cannot feel the rhythm anymore
I want to dance again
and will be content
to hear something as simple
as the song of the flute
from the throat of one small bird.

DONNA DOYLE

A Place We Will Never Be

for Christopher Matthew Elmore
June 6, 1961–August 18, 1991

We won't always be standing
in a grocery store aisle
the night before Thanksgiving,
you removing every egg from the carton,
making sure each one is whole,
needing places you can't see
without looking.

Later, you tell me
you have always wanted
to touch my hair, ask if you can.
Placing unsteady fingers behind my ears,
you pull hesitant handfuls toward light,
watch it fall, each strand becoming
one of those unbroken places you live for.

If hair could save,
your hands would still be traveling mine,
loving a world of silk   light   motion
dancing through your fingers,
a world you had only imagined, like death.
If I had never said: *Yes,*
I would not be here now,
head bowed over a carton of eggs,
holding them one by one,

reassured by unbroken places
I never thought of looking for.

ANGIE VICARS

Saint of Dust

let me in the inner sanctum
if you really have the key
give me, within the walls, a moment
to feast on your divinity
or is it paper
this crown you wear
your wings but shadows
from chains your shoulders bear
what put them there
but the very thin air
of your own despair
I swear
you paint yourself so saintly
and yet you're really coated faintly
with the dust we sinners wear

DORIS IVIE

Father Victor

When but a frightened little boy,
I erected my temple in the wood,
twining building blocks with vines;
by midnight moon I circled it five times,
chanting never there might evil dwell.

Banishing the frightened little boy,
a magician I became, and struck
pentagrams about my windowsills and doors,
encircled myself with fiery Rosy Cross,
commanding evil never there to dwell.

Honoring now the frightened little boy,
a priest I am, and focused on Our Lord.
The Christ I serve and celebrate His Mass.
My Will He took, so now my heart flies free,
believing now that evil never here may dwell.

So mote it be. Le olahm. Amin.

JEAN MARIE WEBB

Black Angel

Black beads, strung seeds
      crucifix hanging on plumb line
           from roped waist

layers, more layers
      smooth black cotton
           concealing black boots

cornice covering forehead
      white hood hiding lean neck
           pressboard over curves

but bisque face revealed,
      and fingers, wedding band,
           groom Jesus

my lungs full of incense,
      plaid heap on marble floor,
           you carried me

wrapped me in black folds,
      wiped my white-laced brow
           with wet cold brown paper

this was our routine

Jesus placed on pupil tongues
      while you sang for me
           in stained-glass bathroom

"dona nobis pacem, pacem"

Black Angel
      I wanted to be like you
           I wanted to be you

wife of Jesus

Now you sing in jungles
       blessing serpents of New Guinea
              catching children as they fall

wiping bronzed brows.
       I want to see you
              I want to be with you

Sister Suzanna,
       I never asked,
              What color was your hair?

JAMEKA RACINTA YOUNG

Rose in the Garden

Easter springs thoughts of new flowers,
bunnies, candy,
and my grandmother's card,
proclaiming, "He is Risen!"
Tucked inside, her note says,
"You can wear white shoes now, dear."
This Easter we ate chocolates in the rain
on the way to church.
My little brother chewed his thumb.

In the afternoon, we planted our dog Rose
underneath the oak in the flower bed.
Daddy dug dark, brown shovelfuls
until a gentle hollow.
We tucked her in, careful to arrange her
comfortably.
I leaned forward
stroked one last time her floppy ears,
told her confidentially, "Here Rosey, your Glowworm."
The Glowworm is chewed, loved.

Whispering softly, my little brother covered her.
"This is the best blanket, Rose. It's soft,"
he whispered.
I remember him, a toddler,
holding his blanket close as he poked
Rose's swollen belly.
She lay patiently on the bed in the white kitchen,
eyes closed, Glowworm beside her.
"Look Mommy, Rose is growing puppies."

There won't be any more puppies.
Maybe wildflowers, or roses.
As Daddy's dirt turns off the light of the yellow blanket,
we water our faces, hands and, finally,
the ground.

Honorable Mention
Young Writer's Prize

WILLIAM H. P. NEVILS

Commemoration of the Octave

It was the Octave of Spring Birds,
the Greening pommeled the earth,
and we lay as lovers lie
in the Name of that which was
and is and will be again.
You said, "I must go,"
and in your saying struck me old,
older than any April I would ever see;
and in your going left me there,
Death and I,
lying close and cold as distant lovers lie
in the Name of that which was
and irrevocable as Infinite is.
Of heaven or hell what is left to know?
Know what the stones themselves
will not leave untold:
There was an Octave of Spring Birds
when the Greening pommeled the earth.

DONNA DOYLE

Left Living

Death makes us larger,
eight settings at the table now,
instead of four.
Together we consume
like only those left living can,
savoring each mouthful,
because we are able,
knowing hunger is proof
the body will not leave the soul alone.

What begins as emptiness
fills us
until we can fill ourselves, each other.
Daughters, wives, sons,
we have lived with grief's not wanting.
Now we live with the intensity of survivors,
laughing harder,
giving deeper,
quiet when we drive past the cemetery:
paper lanterns glow on the hillside,
lights of the dead
shining in the grass like stars.

ELIZABETH HOWARD

Candle of Grief

Like prayer
candles
in a church,
or eternal
flames
at Arlington
or Atlanta,
this white
taper burning
by your picture
is my candle
of grief.
It flickers
in counterpoint
to the tinkle
of sleet,
captures
butterflies
dancing
in the ancient
blue bowl,
but the icy
wind of time
flings open
the door,
and the aura
of butterflies
flutters
into the night.

Susie Sims Irvin

Wailing Wall

I carried your name...to the wall...with the others
coiled like a spring...in the catacombs...of my brain
over continents...through customs...the Zion Gate
down stone alleys...Herod's walled city...Via Dolorosa
past excavation...crumbling cup...brittle bone
Great Portico...approach to...Solomon's Temple
colossal columns...defying...the viewfinder
To the Dung Gate...confronting the...Wailing Wall

On the Men's Side	On the Women's Side
beyond barbed wire Orthodox flutter	I approach as a bride
coattails flapping	fearfully holding to
blackbirds flying in the roost	my father's freckled arm
topknots bob	eyes glued upon the altar
pecking prayers into stone	my single stone
all now cast in violet shadow	magnified menacing baseboard
final focussing of this day.	stripped to bare clay.
	I face my faith.

Nineteen stones below, Jesus stood walked cleared the Temple.
My life gushes before me. a tidal wave splashing stone. recedes.
names come reluctantly. tin scraped from tongue onto impervious stone
the past falls from my fingertips released as a forgotten toy
                    clanging to pavement.

"Why are you here?" "What did you bring?" asks the Wall.
no EXIT sign. no detour arrow. This is the ultimate Wall.
the pitted centuries...crevices crammed. thin rolled prayer petitions.
reminders to God of His promises...

At my side other tongues taste their tears
    one rocking stretches an embroidered apron
        across a bloated belly.
    one pacing, stringy ringlets dripping sweat
        down dusty boots and into cobblestone.

Now. Now your names ring as chimes...coming in clearly...in your own voices
from nursing homes...tennis courts...Kroger's...the supper tables...
I listen...you call your name...and others I had forgotten...
You stand beside me...behind me...I am no longer afraid...not alone...
in my faith...The stone...no barrier now...advances...taking me in.
Suspended there...tightly tenderly held...I leave your name inside.

149

ANN E. THOMPSON

Glass Casket

Flies rest in the glass casket
of the frosted light fixture.
Perpetual sunbathers,
basking in GE's glow.

They have reached their destination
and lie motionless on their backs.
Their god asks for no confessions
or nervous pleas to lie in his vigil.

I stare up at their New Jerusalem,
trying to connect the speckles
curdled on the ceiling
into discovered words, figures.

DONNA DOYLE

Words and Spirit and Flesh

God must be a woman, you tell me,
explaining your aunt's brain tumor,
your first lover leaving you.
Only a woman would inflict
such pain on you, on the world.
Words I have sent your way,
have you heard them?
Late nights over the telephone,
words echoing off your silence,
your silence.
Listen
to my slow drawl,
words you have made fun of,
stories taking you down to the floor,
holding your stomach in laughter.

I can't tell you what God is,
but I know cancer,
I know flesh.
It eats away at more than the flesh,
and the flesh, are you listening?
The flesh does not want to let go.
I am a woman,
flesh caressed, spirit waiting.
I have touched flesh
that did not want to let go.
I would have eaten cancer,
if I could find its heart,
consume the enemy
so its strength would be mine.
Here, I am giving you my voice,
honey
and fire
and birds flying in the rain.
My voice,
to suck on,
to swallow, swallow hard,
to carry inside you
wrapped around that place
hunger never touches.
I am not a god.
I am a woman.
In communion,
I am giving you my voice.

GEORGE SCARBROUGH

Old Men

for Bob Cumming

They lied
When they said
Old men don't rage
At passing strangers
Who once stopped
To adore them:

Calling to account
The straight face,
The look away from
Corners passionate
Cells have been let
To thrive in.

Oh, but they lied
In their good teeth,
Not knowing that old men
Fulminate against
The final, perfect
Adoration.

KAY NEWTON

Writers' Group

for Libba

The sun was going down
when you were here the last time
but the rocks released their heat
and we were warm enough.
Eli and Terry got the giggles.
George hesitated, pointing at the chaise:
"I'm afraid if I sit down there
I never will get up."
"I'll get you up," I promised,
"and while you're there
I'll get you anything you want."
But it was Terry
who spread cream cheese
on hot pretzels for him,
and it was Eli
who refreshed his wine.
When he complained of growing old
you shook your finger in his face:
"*You* hush," you said. "*I'm* dying!"
And after talk of scars, and laughter,
new work shared, admired and criticized,
after we'd made jokes enough
to put death in his puny place,
we rose. You turned to me,
imperious as the *Lion in Winter* queen,
and said, "Remember, Kay:
I'm the one that got George up—
not you." I'll give you that,
just as I'd always give you
anything I had to keep you near.
Now that you're gone
we're left to get each other up
and keep ourselves there.
The water hits the rocks then hits the water,

splashes on itself just as it has on any day
from the beginning;
the fish have fattened, grown,
and multiplied; the weeping cherry
drops its blossoms on the pond,
a pair of cardinals—grandkids, maybe,
of the ones we saw, grown now and mating—
dip and drink and cock a watchful eye
and flit away. It's easier each time we meet;
we don't complain. Stars of Bethlehem
spring from the earth in crevices
between the rocks that still release
their heat. We're warm enough.

LIBBA MOORE GRAY

For an Artist

The creative act starts in the dark
    in a void
    a nothingness
    a not yet
    a no
    a loneliness
from insanity
from the man
the woman
an innocent
a child
and from the darkness
spins a small silver thread
weaving and webbing
until it hangs done
and light shines behind
and through a design
fragility too soon undone
by the stroke of a branch
or a brush

swept down
to the ground
waterdrops on web
rainbows
are scattered and gone
and it starts all over
  in the dark
  in a void
  a nothingness
  a not yet
  a no
  a loneliness
and the form
is a fossil in a rock
handprint
footprint
hidden deep in a cave
underground
unearthed
by a man
or a woman
or a child
and flung in the ocean
like a star falling down
burning a path
through the dark
where it sinks
and finds rest in the sand
and is washed up again
by a current that is felt
but not seen

JUDY LOEST

Remembering Nan

Last summer you buoyed us up with your saucy hats
And Vidalian tongue, waving that feisty fan
In front of the gods—we were sure you were one.
In the winter we kept a map in our heads
Marking your battles and holding our breath
As you came out scarred, but never, never undone.

In the spring we left hyacinths on your doorstep,
Amulets in your mailbox, and an arsenal of books
'Round your bed, loaded and cocked and smoking with Truth.
Still you laughed, and drew us like seekers to Delphi,
In hope and awe, and made us forget for a while
That you were the one with the most to lose.

In May you taught us the Greek dance,
And bought a whole new wardrobe you wore like armor.
We dared not believe you wouldn't survive,
You, with your new-grown hair and full-throated laugh,
Filled with fire and armed to the teeth with love,
The only one among us who seemed truly alive.

You calmed and sustained us and made us believe
We could be like you, fearless and true, might have some
Of what we loved and envied most, a hint
Of what the Greeks call kefi; and that some day, we, too,
Might thrust a defiant fist into the air and say
"Come and get me, I dare you," and win.

In June you sailed on wooden ships to Santorini,
Your beloved white isle in the Aegean Sea, a gift
Funded in love we thought would surely be enough
To hold you. But this time, you walked with labored breath
And swam the blue waters with wounds in your chest
And the Dark Angel never far behind, calling your bluff.

We realized not even love could ever be enough, not for one
As brightly lit as you. Not that Berkeley child
In the photograph with Viking braids and a world to change,
And worlds beyond this. It is fall, and even in death
You distract us in our grief with your unquenchable light
Like the leaf that curls in on itself even as it flames.

Still, we grieve, and smile to find you unexpectedly
In all our measured days of green and gold and gray,
To remember you in dance and rhyme and hyacinth,
To hear you admonish us, "Carpe diem, goddammit!"
And know, again and again, that it was you all along
Who was leaving gifts and teaching us how to live.

CHARLOTTE PENCE

Procession After the Funeral

Now that he's gone,
I awake into the early morning alone.
Weave between the cat mewing, coffee brewing
and live the next hours
the same,
just alone.

Slowly, without me noticing
like the slipping of winter through autumn,
my radio hosts were replaced
by his favorite shows
in languages I don't even know.
I washed the pasture-green curtains, ripped quilts, paint rags,
    handkerchiefs even.
But left his clothes, sweated with aspen scent
in my daily path.
And now throw together dinner with a hammer and chocolate chunks
forgetting my classes on making fresh pasta dough
so tenderly rolled, filled, and flecked with oregano I had grown.

And when another day has come and gone,
I slip to the cool sheets
and can laugh at his mess,
pretentious shows,
smile at what he used to do
still does, just through me, not so alone.

ARTHUR SMITH

Good Deeds

It's easy to forget
This is the bathtub she once drew
Hot water in
And undressed me for
And into which I pooled myself
After a long, down day's work.
How sweet, I remember, scrubbing
At a stubborn spot, and rinsing,
And scrubbing again,
And what generosity that night
As she washed me and dried me
And joined me in bed.

Now when I think of her, I see
A woman asking the man she loves
If she were beautiful,
And I see the man she loves
Saying nothing, believing she were the one
Tried by that question.
A good number of down days would pass
Before his knowing
The difference, before his saying
She was beautiful, to himself aloud,
And again, for good measure,
To the tub.

AMANDA EASTERDAY

Tombstones

I have this
Sudden urge to
leap over
  Tombstones in
the undertones of
  The real moonlight
to feel cool wet
    grass
and look up to see
  the moon watching
me like a painted eye,
  a masterpiece
feel the cold marble
    against my clammy
hands as I thread
  my way through
a night full of
    pale shadows and
loss
sit down on moist
earth and feel
myself go down
to discuss matters
with people no longer
  of this world
They are the ones
who haunt me in my
    dreams, grinning
  toothy, soulful
smiles dancing
inviting me to join
  them
at the first hint of
  light, as shadows
deepen, they disappear
and I am left alone
  with handfuls of
  Dirt.

Honorable Mention
Young Writer's Prize

160

LINDA PARSONS

The Work of the Living

While you're so ill, I should take
small, humble steps, walking head down
in low light. Avoiding words like
never see you again, for to say them
might make it so.

I should set out despite the frozen field,
the winter woods hiding the hunters.
I should do the work of the living
and offer blue beech to the cold hearth,
nursing it through the darkness
with hardly a sound.

I should make lemon tarts, adding
the zest, forming the fleshy cups
into tins black from the fire.
I should not cry out when juice
stings the open places. The table is set
with the yellow demitasse you gave me,
filled to overflowing.

I should remember the little chocolates
the Christmas you took me in. That fall
you dreamed I was feeding you, and nothing
was salty or sweet. I should move my bed
next to yours and dream of truffles,
hardly making a sound.

I should think of you tempered in fire,
on a hillside daring the weather
to worsen. Or melting the January ground,
closing all the open places.
I should think of you going out
to meet spring in the most ordinary ways,
doing the work of the living
in your rose bed, your kitchen,
your days filled to overflowing.

JEFF DANIEL MARION

After a Long Absence
the Chinese Poet
Welcomes His Love
Back to His House
by the River

for Linda

We sip tea, amber as winter dusk
to warm our bones.
Tell me, love, what fortune
you read in the leaves, what future
stirs in the steam and aroma
of this brewing?

The teakettle whistles its old tune,
happy to see us together again.

Outside the wind is wooing
March in, last of winter's daughters,
the shy one with jonquils in her hair.

What is our life but a thousand
glorious yesterdays strewn like leaves
along our path, slender bamboo swaying
as we pass?

Come, let us walk in the grace
of this day, blessed by the sycamores
lifting long arms to the sandhill cranes
whose dance of love we watch
across the river. They call to one another
and rise, outstretched wings to receive
the sky, higher and farther until they disappear
beyond the horizon, some far shore
where they wait for us
already in the future.

ROBERT CUMMING

Creativity

In homage to John Milton

When I consider how the spark is born
so phoenixlike, from cinders of a past
that wandered, undistinguished, worry-worn
from place to place and time to time, at last
it's clear that nothing quite explains the blast
of lustrous words that sets the world ablaze.
The mystery takes our breath; we stand aghast
and look to masters, trying to appraise
a youthful Dylan's alcoholic haze
and see a tortured dreamscape ripe for gleaning,
but filtered through his dark unsteady gaze
the music of the words produced the meaning.
What drove those churning words along? We see
he wrote not poems, only poetry!

LIBBA MOORE GRAY

When I Die

When I die
I will dance
just above the horizon
with everything
patched and mended
where nothing hurts
anymore
and breasts and legs
break through clouds
to the beat of thunder
and the shine of
lightning
where blue jays wing
pirouettes with
sparrows
and rainbows ring my
wrists and head
and dolphins will rise
up
leaping and
somersaulting
all around me
ocean waves will clap
wildly
while I bow
and the mountains bow
and I blow kisses
to the earth
and give God
permission
to draw the curtain
all the time shouting—
"It was good Lord
it was good."

This poem previously appeared in *The Knoxville News-Sentinel* on June 4, 1995.

CONTRIBUTORS

PAT BENJAMIN lives in Oak Ridge and freelances for local newspapers. She has been a frequent winner in Tennessee Poetry Society contests and recently placed in a national contest sponsored by Grandmother Earth Creations.

DAVID BOOKER is an editor for *Log Homes Illustrated* and lives in Knoxville.

BILL BROWN teaches literature and creative writing in Nashville. His third collection of poems, *The Art of Dying*, is recently out from Sow's Ear Press in Virginia. His work has appeared in *Southern Poetry Review, Cumberland Poetry Review, Zone 3, Negative Capability,* and *The English Journal,* among others. In 1995 he received a literary fellowship from the Tennessee Arts Commission and the Distinguished Teacher in the Arts Award from the National Foundation for the Advancement of the Arts. He and his wife tend an orchard, bird watch, and trout fish in Greenbrier, Tennessee.

JULIA BROWN is originally from Rahway, New Jersey, and has been writing poetry since she was 12. She will graduate this fall from Pellissippi State Technical Community College with an Associates of Science degree with an emphasis in communication/journalism. Her poetry has appeared in Mars Hill College's *Cadenza* and in Pellissippi's *Pellissippi Footnotes.* Last year she was editor-in-chief of Pellissippi's newspaper *The Student Voice.*

MATT BROWN is a native of Huntington, West Virginia, and a 1994 graduate in architecture from the University of Tennessee, Knoxville. His poems have appeared locally. He believes that poetry surrounds everyone—we need only to become aware.

JANE CALFEE spent her childhood in whatever locale the U.S. Army dictated, including Nebraska and Okinawa. She has continued to migrate periodically, teaching at the University of San Francisco, Virginia Intermont, Auburn, and now at UT Knoxville for longer than she wants to consider. She has also been an editor, administrator, and dog trainer and is happiest doing whatever leaves her time and energy to write.

JEFF CALLAHAN teaches English, journalism, and creative writing at Farragut High School in Knoxville, where he lives with his wife and three children. His work has appeared in *The Asheville Poetry Review, The Denver Quarterly, Intro, WIND/Literary Journal, Embers,* and *HomeWorks: A Book of Tennessee Writers.*

SANDRA CANNON is a teacher who works for Roane State Community College through the Job Training Partnership Act program in Blount County and teaches GED classes. She also writes scripts for the Black Family Achievement Awards program. She is working on a series of novellas about historically black colleges and universities.

LISA COFFMAN received the 1995 Wick Poetry Prize from Kent State University, which includes the publication of her first book, *Likely*. She was also awarded a Pew Fellowship in the Arts and a Pennsylvania Council Grant for Poetry. She served as resident poet at Bucknell University and studied at UT Knoxville and New York University. Her book contains poems written on the Pew Fellowship about her mother's hometown, Glenmary, Tennessee. She lives and works in Pennsylvania.

ROBERT CUMMING is editor/publisher of the literary publishing house Iris Press, which he recently acquired. He is senior editor of the international scientific journal *Risk Analysis*. His nonfiction has appeared in various journals and his poems have appeared in *The Asheville Poetry Review, Wind,* and *A Gathering at the Forks*. He lives in Oak Ridge, where he is also a health and environmental risk consultant.

HEATHER DOBBINS, originally from Memphis, is a senior in the College Scholars Program at the University of Tennessee, Knoxville. She won UT's Knickerbocker Prize in 1995 and the Margaret Woodruff Award in 1996. She is currently studying in the Netherlands and will pursue an MFA after graduation.

DONNA DOYLE received a BA in English from the University of Tennessee, Knoxville, where she won the Knickerbocker, Woodruff, and UT Women's Coordinating Council awards in poetry. Her poems have appeared in *Coffeehouse Poet's Quarterly, Phoenix Literary Arts Magazine,* and *Miriam Press*. She is a native Knoxvillian.

AMANDA EASTERDAY attends Powell High School in Powell, Tennessee. She enjoys reading, writing poetry, trying to play an out-of-tune guitar, and making her own clothes. She refinishes furniture in a shop in Powell.

EDYE ELLIS hosts two shows for Home and Garden Television—*The Good Life* and *Today at Home*. She was a news anchor for the NBC affiliate in Knoxville for 13 years. Before her career in television, she worked as a print editor and preschool teacher in her hometown, Chicago. Recently she and her mother self-published a small collection of their poems, *Pages*. She believes passionately that poetry comes to life when read aloud and is proud to be included among so many fine voices of the valley.

DOROTHY FOLTZ-GRAY is a past recipient of the Tennessee Arts Commission's Literary Fellowship in Poetry and the Poetry Society of America's award for narrative poetry. Her poems have appeared in numerous publications, including *Mississippi Review*, *Chicago Review*, and *HomeWorks: A Book of Tennessee Writers*. Currently a freelance writer for magazines such as *Parenting* and *Health*, she lives in Knoxville with her husband and two sons.

EDWARD FRANCISCO's collection *L(ie)fe Boat* won the 1994 poetry chapbook competition from Bluestone Press in Massachusetts. His poems have appeared in *Southern Poetry Review*, *Kansas Quarterly*, *International Poetry Review*, and *Negative Capability*, among others. He was a Poet/Scholar for the Voices and Visions Poetry Project sponsored by the National Endowment for the Humanities and the American Library Association.

DORIS GOVE is a biologist and freelance writer living in Knoxville. She has published four books for children on how animals live in their environments. She wants her writing to encourage an understanding of the wonderful diversity of the natural world. She is working on biographies of skinks and fence lizards and an autobiography of a copperhead. This is her first published poem.

JESSE GRAVES grew up on a farm in Sharp's Chapel, Tennessee, and goes home as often as possible. He studies English at the University of Tennessee, Knoxville. The poem in this volume is for his father and Uncle Gerald, who have worked hard in their lives.

JULIANA GRAY, an Alabama native, is in the Master's program in English at the University of Tennessee, Knoxville. She plans to pursue a Ph.D. in writing.

LIBBA MOORE GRAY provided a guiding light to many in the Knoxville Writers' Guild and beyond with her grace, talent, and will to survive. She leaves a legacy of beauty and humor, with six children's books published since 1993 and more scheduled for release, as well as published and unpublished poems and stories. She is greatly missed.

CONNIE JORDAN GREEN writes poetry, a newspaper column, and novels and stories for young people. Her novel *The War at Home* was named an ALA Best Books for Young Adults, and *Emmy* was a Notable 1992 Children's Trade Book in the Field of Social Studies, among other awards. Her poetry has appeared in publications such as *Cumberland Poetry Review, Now & Then, Iowa Woman, HomeWorks: A Book of Tennessee Writers*, and *Voices from the Valley*. She teaches writing at UT Knoxville and at various workshops. She lives on a farm in Loudon County with her husband and thoroughly enjoys her three grandchildren.

JEREMIAH GREEN is a recent graduate of Anderson County High School in Clinton, Tennessee.

BRIAN GRIFFIN received the 1996 Mary McCarthy Award for Short Fiction for his collection *Training To Be an Astronaut*, which will be published by Sarabande Books in 1997. His work has appeared in numerous literary journals, including *Southern Review, Shenandoah*, and *Mississippi Review*. He teaches creative writing in the UT Evening School.

LT. COL. JOHN GROSS is a native of Bristol, Virginia, who served as a platoon leader and company commander in the 9th Infantry Division in Vietnam. He retired from the army in 1988 after 23 years of service. He teaches junior ROTC in Rutledge and lives with his wife Kaye and stepdaughter Hilary in Knoxville.

LINDA LEE HARPER won the 1995 Word Works Washington Prize for Poetry, which included the publication of her first full-length book, *Toward Desire*. Her second book, *Blue Flute*, is forthcoming from Adastra Press. Her poems have appeared in *The Georgia Review, Passages North, The Massachusetts Review, International Quarterly, The Antigonish Review*, and *Kansas Quarterly*, among others. She received fellowships at Yaddo and the Virginia Center for Creative Arts and has taught at the University of Pittsburgh and University of South Carolina at Aiken. Also, she served as editor of *The Pennsylvania Review* and *The Devil's Millhopper* poetry journal. She lives in Knoxville with her husband and her children Kate and Ben.

IRA HARRISON is associate professor of anthropology at the University of Tennessee, Knoxville and serves on the editorial staff of *Medical Anthropology Quarterly*. He has written three books of poetry and reads frequently at benefits for civil rights and women's health issues. His work also appears in *HomeWorks: A Book of Tennessee Writers*.

DEBBIE PATTON HOLLENBECK has been in the printing business over 16 years and is currently in sales for EBSCO Media. She serves on the board and as secretary for the Knoxville Writers' Guild. Her fiction appears in *Voices from the Valley.*

ELIZABETH HOWARD lives in Crossville and is a frequent winner in contests sponsored by the Tennessee Mountain Writers' Conference, Cookeville Creative Writers' Association, and Mid-South Writers' Association, among others. Her poems have appeared, or are forthcoming, in *Appalachian Heritage, Now & Then, Wind,* and *Potato Eyes.* She has an MA in English from Vanderbilt University.

DAVID HUNTER, born and raised in north Knox County, is proud to be a hillbilly to the bone. He has worked variously as an iron worker, ditch digger, soldier, truck driver, doughnut maker, police officer, and newspaper columnist. He has eight published books—two novels and six works of nonfiction. He is at work on the third part of his memoirs, and a new novel is forthcoming from New Messenger Books.

JOHN IRVIN is a recent graduate of West High School in Knoxville and plans to study drama and literature at UT Knoxville. The poem in this volume represents his growing spiritual awareness of the importance of peace and unity among all peoples.

SUSIE SIMS IRVIN writes about her Middle Tennessee upbringing, rural life in Williamson County, the town of Franklin, and travels beyond. Her inspirational writing has appeared in *The Old Hickory Review* and in United Methodist literature and has won contests sponsored by the Cookeville Creative Writers' Association and Corbow Press in Georgia.

DORIS IVIE is an educational psychologist and professor and program coordinator in psychology at Pellissippi State Technical Community College. Her poems, book reviews, and articles have appeared in a variety of publications. She has traveled extensively but chooses to live and work in Knoxville, her hometown. Her poetry is an intricate part of the spiritual fabric of her life.

JAMES B. JOHNSTON, a native of Belfast, Northern Ireland, graduated from Trinity College in Dublin. He and his wife emigrated to Ontario in 1974. He and his family relocated to Alabama in 1984 and to Knoxville in 1990. He founded Celtic Cat Publishing in 1995 and is working on his first book of poems.

MARILYN KALLET is professor of English and director of the Creative Writing Program at the University of Tennessee, Knoxville. As poet, translator, essayist, and editor, she has authored six books, including *A House of Gathering: Poets on May Sarton's Poetry* (1993). She is widely published and in 1988 won the Tennessee Arts Commission's Literary Fellowship in Poetry. She co-edits *Worlds in Our Words: Contemporary American Women Writers*, forthcoming from Blair Press/Prentice Hall.

LESLIE LACHANCE, a former New Yorker, landed on her feet in Knoxville in 1991, dialectically confused but well intentioned. She can cook a pretty good garlic and hot pepper spaghetti sauce and enjoys performing opera librettos to the tune of "Three Blind Mice."

DAVID LAUVER has worked as a corporate speechwriter and communications manager, university public relations director, U.S. Senate press and legislative assistant, and newspaper reporter. He is a published songwriter and four-time finalist in the national songwriting competition held in conjunction with North Carolina's Merle Watson Festival.

JUDY LOEST, a Virginia native, is in the Master's program in English at the University of Tennessee, Knoxville. She dabbles at poetry and painting and is a confirmed bibliophage/phile.

JEFF DANIEL MARION is poet-in-residence and director of the Appalachian Center at Carson-Newman College. His work has appeared in *The Southern Poetry Review, Zone 3*, and *Appalachia Inside Out*, among others. In 1978 he received the first Tennessee Arts Commission Literary Fellowship in Poetry. Recent books are *Lost & Found* (1994), his fourth poetry collection, and a children's book, *Hello, Crow* (1992). In 1993 he participated in an Audience Development Grant sponsored by the National Endowment for the Arts in conjunction with UT Knoxville. His achievements were honored at Emory & Henry College's 1994 Literary Festival. He lives on the banks of the Holston River, where his work continues to embody the importance of place in a writer's life.

EARLINE MCCLAIN has had a long teaching career in Knox and Sevier County schools. She also taught and directed education programs at Knoxville College for twenty years. Writing for her is a source of joy, a reliever of stress, and a thrilling compulsion.

JENNIFER MCKAIG is a recent graduate from Oak Ridge High School. As the daughter of missionaries, she was born in Germany and lived in three countries by age 11. She has also moved around quite a bit in the U.S. Writing gives her a sense of release, perspective, and sanctuary in a life that has often been disrupted. She plans to attend UT Knoxville.

FLORENCE MCNABB lives in Knoxville with her daughter, two dogs, and two cats. Her poems have appeared in *Now & Then* and *Voices from the Valley.* She is a bookseller at Davis-Kidd Booksellers.

LAUREL MCNEELEY, a Knoxville native, is a second-year student at the University of Virginia where she is studying art history and English. She hopes to pursue a career involving poetry.

JENNY NASH is a freelance writer living in Knoxville with her family. She has written for *Storytelling* magazine and the Home and Garden Television program guide. These are her first published poems.

ACEY NEEL is a senior at Oak Ridge High School and a native of South Carolina. A member of the Oak Ridge Rowing Association Varsity Girls' Crew, she was the only rower from Tennessee invited to participate in the Junior National Team selection camp at Dartmouth College. She hopes to represent the U.S. at the World Championships in Scotland.

WILLIAM H. P. NEVILS is an Episcopal priest in the Diocese of East Tennessee who lives in Tazewell. He oversees two parishes, in Rogersville and LaFollette, and chairs Genesis, a rural organizing project for five East Tennessee counties. He is also active in several Tennessee historical societies.

KAY NEWTON runs a small bed and breakfast in the heart of Knoxville, which provides plenty of material for her to write poetry, fiction, drama, and songs without feeling the need to push herself to publish. She has a whole suitcase of song lyrics, in case anyone wants to make her an offer.

CAROLINE NORRIS is a Boston native who has lived in Brooklyn, Chicago, Paris, Yokohama, St. Louis and, for many years, in the Hudson River valley above New York City. She now lives in Maryville, Tennessee, by a stream, and is a career consultant and college English instructor.

SUE RICHARDSON ORR and her husband own and operate Orr Mountain Winery in Madisonville, Tennessee. Her nonfiction has won awards at the 1996 and 1995 Tennessee Mountain Writers' Conference. Her poetry has appeared in *Coping* magazine.

LINDA PARSONS, a native Nashvillian, is poetry editor of *Now & Then* magazine, published by the Center for Appalachian Studies and Services at East Tennessee State University. She received a 1996–97 literary fellowship from the Tennessee Arts Commission, among other awards. Her poems have appeared in publications such as *The Georgia Review, The Iowa Review, Prairie Schooner, The Asheville Poetry Review, Helicon Nine, Negative Capability, Kalliope,* and *HomeWorks: A Book of Tennessee Writers.* She contributes a regular column to *New Millennium Writings.* Her first book of poems, *Home Fires,* is forthcoming from Sow's Ear Press in Virginia. Midwifing this anthology has been her labor of love.

RICHARD J. PATTON wrote the poem in this volume for Pellissippi State Technical Community College's 1996 Earth Day celebration. It is his first published poem. He is an adjunct professor of English at Pellissippi and acts in local theatre productions. He has also published literary criticism and nonfiction.

CHARLOTTE PENCE, a recent graduate of UT Knoxville, studied international relations, English, and Spanish. She is working on her MFA in creative writing at Emerson College in Boston. Her poetry has appeared in national publications such as *The Christian Science Monitor.*

172

LEAH PREWITT is a native of Lexington, Kentucky, and the chief federal defender of East Tennessee. She was a finalist for the 1995 Robert Penn Warren Poetry Prize. Her work has appeared in *Cumberland Poetry Review* and *Now & Then.*

ROSE BECALLO RANEY completed her MA in English with an emphasis in creative writing in 1992 at UT Knoxville, where she won the 1991 and 1992 graduate awards for poetry and fiction, respectively. She was one of two first-place winners in the 1994 Tennessee Writers Alliance poetry competition. She enjoys writing poetry with lyrical and formal qualities. She is a senior technical writer and editor for a scientific and engineering management firm in Oak Ridge and lives in Knoxville with her husband Chris and her son Zachary.

CANDANCE W. REAVES is an assistant professor of English at Pellissippi State Technical Community College where she teaches creative writing and other English courses. She placed second in the 1994 Tennessee Writers Alliance poetry competition. Her poems appear in *HomeWorks: A Book of Tennessee Writers* and *Voices from the Valley.* She is grateful to have been born in an area so rich with poetry and so blessed with those brave enough to capture it.

DANIEL ROOP is from Powell, Tennessee. He loves reading and writing poetry. He tries very hard, but not hard enough (or so he says).

DON SCALF has published fiction and nonfiction since 1979. His short stories have appeared in *Rural Heritage, Hometown Press*, and *Rural Living*, among other journals and anthologies, and he has won numerous literary prizes in the South. He works as an environmental technical writer and lives on the banks of the Tennessee River, where he is at work on his sixth novel.

DEBORAH SCAPEROTH holds an MA in English from East Tennessee State University and is an adjunct instructor in the UT English department. She has taught at the University of Memphis and Columbus State in Columbus, Ohio. She lives in Knoxville with her children David, Elizabeth, and Matt and her husband Daniel, a radiation oncologist at the Thompson Cancer Survival Center.

GEORGE SCARBROUGH, a native of Polk County, Tennessee, has published in the country's most prestigious magazines. His work includes five volumes of poetry and one novel. His latest collection of poetry, *Invitation to Kim*, was nominated for a Pulitzer Prize in 1990. He lives and writes in Oak Ridge, Tennessee.

LINDA SCHAIBLE is a graduate of the University of New Orleans. She won the 1994 Bain-Swiggett Poetry Prize and performs with the songwriting duo Amelia Earhart Returns. She lives in Knoxville and is the market research coordinator for Computational Systems, Inc.

JOAN SHROYER-KENO was the first runner-up for the 1995 Coos Bay Writers Workshop—Mary Scheirman Poetry Award. Her poetry has appeared in various small press journals and anthologies. She recently moved to Dryden, New York.

ARTHUR SMITH was born and raised in central California. His first book of poems, *Elegy on Independence Day*, received the Agnes Lynch Starrett Poetry Prize and publication by the University of Pittsburgh Press in 1985. The book was selected by the Poetry Society of America to receive the Norma Farber First Book Award. He also received a National Endowment for the Arts Creative Writing Fellowship and two Pushcart Prizes and was selected as the Theodore Morrison Fellow in Poetry for the 1987 Bread Loaf Writer's Conference. He is an associate professor of English at UT Knoxville. His second collection, *Orders of Affection*, is from Carnegie Mellon University Press (1996).

KATHERINE SMITH received her MFA from the University of Virginia in 1985. After spending nine years in France, she has returned to Knoxville with her daughter Justina.

STACY SMITH has published her first book of poems and photography, *Song of the Purple*, with New Messenger Books. She is a recent graduate of UT's Whittle Scholars and College Scholars programs with emphases in creative writing and photography. Her work has appeared in local and international magazines and anthologies. She hopes to pursue advanced degrees in English and teach creative writing.

ART STEWART is an aquatic ecologist and senior scientist at Oak Ridge National Laboratory. His work, which has won regional and national awards, reflects a diverse range of geographic experiences—his childhood in Indiana, college years in Arizona, the Peace Corps in Ghana, graduate studies in Michigan, and research and teaching in Oklahoma before moving to Knoxville.

ANN E. THOMPSON is a native Memphian who received her BA from Arkansas State University. She is currently employed at Goody's Family Clothing as an advertising copywriter.

MELISSA THOMPSON is from New Tazewell and a recent graduate from the University of Tennessee, Knoxville in psychology. She plans to pursue a graduate degree in clinical psychology. She enjoys capturing the richness of her small hometown in her writing and draws upon traditions of her family and fellow East Tennesseans.

HELEN DIACOMICHAL TURLEY has published poetry in *The Texas Quarterly* and fiction in *Voices from the Valley*. In 1988 she received her BA in English from the University of Tennessee, Knoxville and frequently reads her poetry for Knoxville, Clinton, and Oak Ridge audiences. She serves as historian on the board of the Knoxville Writers' Guild.

JENNIFER VASIL is a recent graduate of UT's College Scholars program with emphases in English, creative writing, and Russian translation. She has published poetry in *Phoenix Literary Arts Magazine* and *eNteLechY*. She was a coordinator and workshop presenter at UT's 1996 Young Writers' Institute. She lives in Asheville, where she volunteers at the Western North Carolina Nature Center.

ANGIE VICARS has been writing something or the other for most of her life. Occasionally she took time out to earn degrees. She holds a BA in theatre from the University of Tennessee, Knoxville and an MFA in screenwriting from the University of Miami. She also coordinates events such as the writers' roundtable at Bookstar.

BRAD VICE is a poet and fiction writer from Alabama. His fiction has appeared in *The Georgia Review* and recently won the UT Women's Coordinating Council short story contest. He was nominated for the Ruth Lilly National Collegiate Poetry Award and is working on his Master's in English at UT Knoxville.

JEAN MARIE WEBB is a graduate student at the University of Tennessee, Knoxville in the College of Education. She teaches creative writing to inner-city children in Knoxville and lives in Maryville with her two daughters. This is her first published poem.

DON WILLIAMS is a columnist for *The Knoxville News-Sentinel* and founder of *New Millennium Writings, A Journal for the 21st Century.* He has won a Golden Press Card Award, a Michigan Journalism Fellowship, and awards from the Tennessee Press Association, Associated Press, and Scripps-Howard newspapers. His articles about Libba Moore Gray's battle with breast cancer won the 1995 Malcolm Law Award, the top journalism prize in Tennessee. His journalism and short fiction have been anthologized.

JAMEKA RACINTA YOUNG is a recent graduate of Farragut High School in Knoxville. She has received a scholarship to swim competitively at Transylvania University in Kentucky. She coaches gymnastics and enjoys playing the flute.